The *Life* You Dream of

52 BREAKTHROUGHS TO GET BEYOND
WHAT KEEPS YOU STUCK &
HOLDS YOU BACK

EMILY GOWOR

The Life You Dream Of: 52 Breakthroughs To Get Beyond What Keeps You Stuck & Holds You Back © Emily Gowor 2024

www.emilygowor.com

The moral rights of Emily Gowor to be identified as the author of this work have been asserted in accordance with the Copyright Act 1968.

First published in Australia 2024 by Gowor International Publishing

ISBN 978-0-6455734-6-6

Any opinions expressed in this work are exclusively those of the author and are not necessarily the views held or endorsed by Gowor International Publishing.

All rights reserved. No part of this publication may be reproduced or transmitted by any means, electronic, photocopying or otherwise, without prior written permission of the author.

Disclaimer

All the information, techniques, skills and concepts contained within this publication are of the nature of general comment only and are not in any way recommended as individual advice. The intent is to offer a variety of information to provide a wider range of choices now and in the future, recognising that we all have widely diverse circumstances and viewpoints. Should any reader choose to make use of the information herein, this is their decision, and the author and publisher(s) do not assume any responsibilities whatsoever under any conditions or circumstances. The author does not take responsibility for the business, financial, personal or other success, results, or fulfilment upon the readers' decision to use this information. It is recommended that the reader obtain their own independent advice.

Words Of Acknowledgement For Emily

"Emily, you do amazing work. I just want to say that. If you were not in my life, where would I be? I just need you to know that. Thank you."

Andrea Baumann, Healer & Author

"Emily is an inspirational legend. As a mentor, she will advocate for you, cheer you on, and be completely in your corner. She will walk beside you, guiding and coaching you through all aspects of business and life. I cannot recommend her highly enough, and for myself, she has been the best investment and gift I could have asked for."

Alana Clare Power, Writer & Soul Channel

"I have had the opportunity to be coached by Emily Gowor who provided with me guidance for my new counselling service. Emily took me through all the challenges I struggled with and helped me every step of the way, providing an excellent written plan for me to move ahead. She also assisted in helping to find my true purpose, one that aligns with my gifts and experiences. I am very grateful to have had such an excellent mentor for my journey."

Emilia Bruckner, Counsellor

"I had known Emily for some years before I hired her as a mentor. Emily's enthusiasm and inspiration to help people realise their fullest potential is unbridled and this, coupled with her knowledge of universal principles, makes her unique as a mentor. Not only is Emily helping me to write my book, but she is also helping me set up my business in alignment with my purpose and vision so I can leave my legacy in the world.

Her mentoring style gets to the heart of the matter. She simplifies steps and creates relevant structures and systems to achieve results. I would highly recommend her for anyone wishing to pursue their dreams in a grounded, practical way, yet with inspiration and fulfilment."

DR ERIKA YEATES, LEADERSHIP MENTOR & TRAINER

"Emily is the kind of entrepreneur that people dream of becoming. While most of the business community build their lives around their businesses, I find it refreshing that she managed to build her business around her ideal life. I have bought and read all of her books, and I love her videos. I readily recommend her services whenever I get the chance."

CHRIS HOOPER, ACCOUNTANT, ENTREPRENEUR & KEYNOTE SPEAKER

"I am very proud to be associated with this dynamic lady, whose wisdom greatly exceeds her tender years. She is a role model for people to follow their heart and build a business based on their values and principles. If you are considering Emily as a mentor, then I would recommend her to you, just as I have done with several of my friends and associates. They were impressed, and I promise that you will be too."

TONY INMAN, BUSINESS CONSULTANT

"I worked with Emily for six months. I contacted her as I resonated with her authentic and open communication. Her weekly inspiring tips on YouTube helped me through a time in my life when I was searching for growth. Emily's mentoring helped me build confidence in myself and provided me with the support that I needed to go and action on my dreams.

Too often, I meet people who talk about their dreams but never do anything about them. Emily has a gift to get you going in an inspiring and energising way by closing the gap between what you want and where you're at right now."

MIA MARIA BERGLUND

"Emily is a highly skilled communicator and writer. I have had her on my radio show, and she is highly effective in communicating from the heart and painting beautiful pictures with her words.
I have also read a few of her books and highly recommend her as a keynote speaker. I encourage everyone to purchase and read her books."

BRAD SIMKINS, RADIO SHOW HOST

DEDICATION

This book is dedicated to my long-time mentor Dr John F Demartini for helping me to feel worthy of love and for showing me the true potential that is within me. Your lasting presence in my life reminds me that I am far greater than any circumstance I might face, and that love prevails in all ways.

What would I have done without you?

Life From Above

This book was originally titled *Life From Above* – and here's why.

A few days before I began writing the book, I was on a flight from Brisbane to Melbourne in Australia. I was flying to my birth city for a TV interview on the Global Women Empowerment Show for Channel 31. It was the 2nd of May in 2024 – and it was a *beautiful* day to fly.

After completing an hour of inspired work during the flight, I felt intuitively guided to put my laptop away. I set it to sleep mode, closed the lid, and slid it back into my handbag. Sitting in the window seat, I turned my head to look out at the view below.

As I looked out at the airplane wing, the bright blue sky, and the white clouds, I was overwhelmed by the beauty of the scene before me. Perfectly suspended between the heaven and the Earth, a feeling of deep humility washed over me. I felt the presence of the divine - the higher power that governs all life on the planet - and our unlimited potential to thrive.

Simultaneously, I became aware of the collective struggle that humanity faces day-to-day, and just how weighed down we can become by what is happening in our lives. I felt the presence of our adversities and a glimpse of our greater destiny in the same moment. It was *inspiring*. In that heart-opening moment, I heard the phrase "life from above" in my mind, loud, clear and straight from above.

Tears instantly filled my eyes, and I felt the presence of God. Knowing that I had just been sent the essence, heart, and soul of my next book, I nodded my head towards the sky and said, "Thank you," silently, to acknowledge the gift that I had received.

A few seconds later, I captured the photo that you now see on the front cover. To me, the expansive and inspiring view out over the clouds and across the clear blue sky reflects our extraordinary nature and our ability to transcend our difficulties and let our spirit soar – and it could not be more perfect for this book.

That moment will stay with me for the rest of my life as I hope this book does for you, acting as a constant reminder that you *deserve* more and that you are capable of achieving and experiencing great things during your short flight here.

Although it may feel like it at times, you are not small – you are MIGHTY – and this world benefits immensely from your presence. So, promise me and promise yourself that you will not let that which is trivial interfere with what you feel you were born to do.

It truly is time to fly.

From my heart to yours – Andiamo (let's go!).

Foreword

Let me take this opportunity to introduce you to the most inspirational and soulful human being that I have ever met: Emily Gowor! I believe in angels which means 'messenger' – and I have no doubt that Emily is an angel.

Emily's heart is on fire for humanity. Her gift and mission in life is to change the world, one person at a time, and to inspire people to fulfil their soul's purpose and make their impact. That is Emily's 'message'.

Emily has gone through many ups and downs in her own life, including overcoming near-suicidal depression. Because of her hardship, she devoted herself to becoming a soulful inspirational writer, author and speaker who encourages people to reach their highest potential on the path of their true destiny.

Emily has touched, moved, and inspired me to uncover my own capabilities by encouraging me and supporting me to search deep within myself to discover the real me. She has become one of my treasured mentors, guiding me through my business world and personal life. Her empathy and heartfelt love are undeniable.

Very seldom do you come across a book as rich and as thought-provoking as *The Life You Dream Of*. This inspirational book from Emily reveals a treasure on every page. It is overflowing with love and spiritual wisdom that will guide you to find and fulfil your soul's calling here on Earth. This book will ignite the flame within you and change your life!

Blessings.

Angelika Jankovic-Del Bianco
Author, Speaker & Trainer

PREFACE

As a child and teenager, I spent a great deal of time feeling small on the inside. I was extremely shy in public settings and although I was loved, valued, and believed in by both of my parents, I somehow felt that I was insignificant. On an emotional level – and it was purely my own emotion, not the truth – I felt that I wasn't desirable, cool, or popular. It seemed that I didn't fit in and that I was an awkward outsider.

Because of this, it is no mystery why I entered adulthood focused on and intrigued by the greater potential within us. On a deep subconscious level, I wanted to discover what was beyond external appearances. I wanted to set myself free from the limits I had placed on myself and live from my higher self, my infinite mind, and my transcendent soul.

I was determined to disprove my own beliefs and sell myself a whole new story about who I was. I wanted to discover the truth of my innate worth and value, and even as a teenager, I suspected that there was far more to me than met the eye. I felt drawn to that 'life from above' – a life guided by my spirit, not determined by my wounds. I was driven to unearth and connect with my greatness.

My fascination with human potential, emotions, and the deep world within us hasn't subsided for two decades and, as it turns out, it has been a crucial theme of my life's work here: to discover what we are made of and to understand how to make the most of ourselves and our lives. My devotion to this calling has been alluring and exquisitely profound, bringing with it many unexpected and incredibly moving gifts.

As I look out at the world around me, I am intrigued by what makes people tick. Why do some people rise to the top while others seem to struggle their way through life? What restricts the flow of our innate potential? How do our emotions work and what can we do to master them so that they don't trip us over along the way? What are those invisible barriers that we can't see but that we feel within us? And, most importantly, how can we overcome our limitations so we can live the way I believe we were designed to? What is the key to that expanded life?

On my journey, I was first and foremost on a mission to discover something bigger, grander, and greater within myself: the potential I sensed was within me. I somehow knew that it would help me overcome my human 'stuff' – my perceptions of smallness, my shame, my timidity, and my desire to hide. And secondly, I wanted to share that all-important message with humanity, that as I stated so beautifully in the title of one of my previous books, we are "Born Great" and destined for something far more extraordinary than we often realise or are told.

The enormous potential I have discovered in myself over the years through deep soul-searching, emotional healing, and through living boldly pursuing what I love astounds me. Just how deep my personal transformation has been and what I have achieved in my life so far not only humbles and fills me with deep gratitude, but it proves to me that we *significantly* underestimate who we are and what we can do in this world.

Too often, too many of us are weighed down by the numerous challenges of growing up, of finding ourselves, of building a life, of earning money, of navigating relationships, of discovering our path, and of cultivating a prosperous future. It can feel so overwhelming at times that we can buckle under the pressure of it all. And sadly, and all too often, our dreams go down the drain in the process. But no matter how difficult the path might seem, how trying the current circumstances, or how defeated, lost, and empty we may feel, I *do* believe that there is a way forwards and that we *can* find a way to break through and rise.

Therefore, I have written this book with the intention to provide you with insight about what holds *you* back from the greater life you were born for. It is my wish that it will assist you to identify and transcend what undermines your purpose, your potential, and your dreams. I wrote it because I cannot help but feel that we are far more capable and extraordinary than we often realise, and because nothing would inspire me more than knowing that this book helped you to get out of your own way and experience the magic that life has in store for you.

The older I become, the more precious life feels to me. Achievement and adversity, along with the many chapters of my journey, have taught me that our time here is limited and far shorter than we can comprehend. It goes by *fast* – and if we don't at least try to make the absolute most of our life, we will miss out on so much.

I don't believe that we were put here to suffer or that we *want* to stay small, hold back, and block ourselves at every turn. Instead, I believe that we want to squeeze every drop out of this beautiful gift, use the world as a stage, be who we are, say what we feel, live, try, experiment, experience, grow, heal, and feel as much as humanly possible: to live a life without limits.

We want to feel the fear and do it anyway, to transcend anything that causes us to settle for less than we desire. We want to LIVE fully, boldly, wholly, with an open heart, an open mind, and a lighter spirit. It is my heartfelt wish that this book will inspire you to do just that – and I look forward to hearing about your dreams.

Contents

Words Of Acknowledgement For Emily v

Life From Above xi

Foreword xiii

Preface xv

Introduction 1

1: Dreaming Small 11

2: Aimless Living 17

3: Underestimating Yourself 19

4: Success Guilt 23

5: Spiritual Separation 27

6: Family Imprints 31

7: Uninspiring Influences 35

8: Following The Crowd 40

9: Comparison Obsession 44

10: Hiding Your Gifts 49

11: Always Adulting 53

12: Financial Survival 57

13: Emotional Baggage 61

14: Rescuing Humanity 66

15: Burnout 71

16: Overwhelm 75

17: High-Achiever Syndrome 80

18: Failure Focus 85

19: Low Self-Worth 90

20: Control Complex 95

21: Time Management 99

22: Wishful Thinking 103

23: Relationship Sacrifice 107

24: Extreme Adversity 112

25: Giving Up Early 117

26: Victim Mentality 121

27: Disempowerment 126

28: Ageism 130

29: One-Dimensional Living 134

30: Digital Drowning 138

31: Dodging Discomfort 143

32: Money Repression 148

33: Money Obsession 153

34: Clutter and Chaos 158

35: Approval Addiction 163

36: Poor Health 168

37: Ignoring Inner Guidance 172

38: Shyness 176

39: Creativity Overload 181

40: Overthinking Things 186

41: Undermining Your Dreams 190

42: Flying Solo 194

43: Chasing Destinations 198

44: Blaming and Complaining 202

45: Drama Addiction 206

46: Your Inner Perfectionist 210

47: Fear 214

48: Disconnection From Humanity 218

49: Image Insecurities 222

50: Hugging The Rock 226

51: Low Vibration Living 230

52: Delaying Your Dreams 234

Your Reflection Time 238

53 241

Create Your Breakthrough Plan 245

Conclusion 249

Daydream 258

Acknowledgements 260

About The Author 264

Other Books By Emily 266

Introduction

"Someday - maybe today, maybe tomorrow, or maybe in ten years from now - you will take a step back, evaluate the purpose of your life, and ask yourself the question 'What is it all for?'

My hope is that you will decide to live, love, and work in such a way that at the end of your years, the answer to this question is so profound, so beautiful, and so inspiring that tears roll down your cheeks."

Emily Gowor, Born Great

Too often, we are weighed down by what is happening in our life on Earth. We feel stressed, overwhelmed, anxious, beaten down, challenged, stretched, burned out, drained, or just flat-out broken. We feel lost. We flail and struggle our way through the days, weeks, and years. We become caught in drama, trials, and tests that fill our precious time and consume our valuable energy. We can't see the path forwards and our spirit feels heavy.

Then, we hold back, push back, or give up on our goals and dreams entirely, because life feels hard, and trying to create a life that we love simply feels too difficult. Combine this with the truth that so many of us are obsessively comparing, crushing, judging, and beating ourselves up, and it's a recipe for an unfulfilling life.

And yet we are born for more. SO much more. You were born with extraordinary potential – and I believe that your heart is guiding you to *unlock* it. Every single day, your soul calls out to you, nudging and pulling you to greener pastures, to a life centred around your purpose. Your higher self knows what is possible for you, and when you do break free of whatever hinders you, you will create and experience an everyday reality so inspiring, so extraordinary, so meaningful, so exquisitely beautiful, that it will move you to the core.

I know that you yearn for that profound, powerful, and authentic life. I do, too. That's what this book – and my entire life's work and my heartfelt devotion to inspire people – is for. It is to unleash who you *truly* are and unlock entirely new possibilities for you … because they exist and because you deserve it.

A Journey To Awaken Your Greatness

This book contains my deepest insights about what holds us back, keeps us playing small, and interferes with the manifestation of what we were born for – and what we can do about it. In each chapter, I will share a possible reason that could be distracting or deterring you from moving forward boldly on your path and my perspective on how you might overcome it. My mission is to help you to set yourself free from the human hindrances and baggage that keeps you stuck so that you can reach the fullest expression of your soul's calling.

I have researched, reflected on, and drawn conclusions as to why we don't pursue and fulfil the heartfelt dreams, the inspired visions, and the divine plans that exist within us; the glimpses of our future and of what could be. My insights have been distilled from nearly two decades of meeting people, observing humanity, and mentoring clients, all the while hearing and feeling what *hurts* and *hinders* the life they dream of.

I wanted to know: what creates the gap between where we are and where we want to be? What slows us down from achieving what we dream of? Why do we hold back, put off, or ignore what our heart calls us to do? Why do we earn less money than we desire and keep doing things that drain us instead of pursuing our dreams? Why do we keep what we want just out of our reach and create glass ceilings for ourselves? Why do we allow ourselves to suffer far longer than is necessary in a life we don't *love*? What is all that 'resistance to greatness' really about?

These insights also share personal observations from many years of aspiring for more in my own life. As I have given my dreams my all, I have encountered many an internal obstacle: a 'reason' that I was holding back and doing or saying or trying less than I wanted to, less than I knew I was capable of. These reasons are here within the pages of this book, the invisible obstacles that slowed me down until I unearthed, healed, transformed, and dissolved them.

In business, finance, my career, my health, and my personal life, I have uncovered many a shadow to confront – a cave to enter – each one a golden opportunity to bury the hatchet, let go of what no longer serves, and claim the destiny I yearn for.

That journey never stops because there are always new 'edges' to lean into; new limitations to overcome, new healing to experience, and new accomplishments to reach for. It is in being willing to discover our 'demons', leaning into our discomfort, and taking bold action steps that we create a life transcendent of what would otherwise be our baggage.

How To Use This Book

I certainly cannot say that what I share in this book is definitive or final. There may be reasons you can think of in your life that I haven't written about here, and I am sure that I will discover many more on my own journey. (I have left a space at the end of the book for you to add and explore what you feel has been the biggest barrier to *your* dreams.)

What I do know, however, is that we are all human, and because of this, I am sure that you will be able to relate to several of these limitations that cause unfulfilled potential and unexpressed dreams. In fact, you may discover many of your limits within these pages which may feel confronting at times, and it is for this reason that I don't necessarily recommend reading the book in one sitting. If that occurs, please don't draw the conclusion that you are a complete mess and that you will never achieve your dreams.

Simply write down which reasons you resonated with the most (there is also a page at the end of the book where you can make note of these as you read). This will help you to identify the 'stumbling blocks' you resonate with and decide which hurdles are the next most important ones to overcome for you to take to the skies and flourish in your life.

Some of the causes of unfulfilled dreams that I have written about will require small refinements, daily reminders, or a weekend project to overcome. Others may take weeks, months, or even years of inward reflection and dedicated personal growth work to heal the wounding and shift the psychological patterns that run your life. Either way, it will be worth the effort, because what is on the other side is extraordinary. Life-altering. Mind-blowing. Humbling. Believe me – you won't want to miss it.

You can read this book in whichever way feels best. You might choose to read it front to back, carefully absorbing the ideas one at a time and asking yourself if *this* is *the one* that sets you free, and then marking the topics that struck a chord for you as areas to work on. You might even choose to start a journal practice where you explore one of these 'limiting reasons' per week, writing about it to reflect inwardly and seek new insight.

The other option is to use the book like an oracle card deck. You might pick it up and flick through it randomly, seeing which topic you land on and then carrying that thought with you for the day or week ahead. It is entirely up to you. Use it in whatever way is necessary for your optimal growth.

My goal in sharing each of these insights is to help you unlock YOUR extraordinary nature, one overturned limit at a time: to live a life beyond struggle instead of one where you feel continuously defeated or buried by the challenges you face. It is to help you name and dismantle the subconscious barriers that you seem to run into, the 'blocks' that you cannot see but that you can feel, the ones that seem to prevent you from a life fully lived.

It is to find your fear and face it. To know your own mental and emotional limitations and to move forwards on your path regardless.

To uncover your wounds and heal. To use your adversity as fuel and allow your higher self to get behind your human self so you can rise and thrive. To understand yourself so you can work *with* yourself instead of against yourself – because you *do* love yourself and because you *know* you are capable of MORE.

Deep inside you, you know this is true. You know you aren't here for a cookie-cutter life. You were born for an extraordinary existence: one that is overflowing with everything you love and the very essence of your authentic self. A life that lights you up, a life where you express who you are, a life where you set yourself free. You know you have greatness at your core and the likelihood is that, regardless of how far you have already come on your journey, you can still do, feel, be, become, achieve, experience, and reach so much more in your remaining years – and you deserve to.

I willingly admit that life isn't always easy. In fact, it is the greatest personal development program we ever undertake. Designing our future, building a life, mastering health, wealth, and relationships, experiencing deep meaning, doing something worthwhile, creating a rewarding career, finding a mate, raising a family, mastering our craft, leaving a legacy – this all requires growth. And despite the endless support, signs, confirmations, and the many blessings we experience on our journey, there is no doubt that this growth is rarely smooth.

But you DO have dreams to chase. You DO have a purpose to pursue. And there IS a greater future for you, just waiting to be unlocked, expressed, lived, fulfilled. You can tap into the higher aspect of yourself that knows exactly what you are here to do and what your life is all about – and *listen* to it. You can live from the soul not the senses, from the heart not the fear, from the solution not the struggle, from the opportunity not the burden. You can find your courage in each moment and live greater. You can transcend your challenges, one by one, and live your life by design, not by default. But, you *must* master your inner world before you can master your outer world: your destiny.

Master Your Mind To Master Your Life

There are many self-development and business mentors who say that mindset is 50% of the game when it comes to achieving what we desire in life and taking action is the other half. I tend to agree. However, it is also worth considering that mindset – our inner state of psychology – is, in some senses, 100% of the game.

Why? Because every single action you take, every reaction you have, every decision and every hesitation stems from your state of mind. Without the drive required to push yourself and do big things, you won't tap into your extraordinary abilities. Without the desire to make the most of your life, you won't discover just how beautiful your life could be. Without the yearning to see what you are capable of in the future, you will keep living a life based on the past.

Looking at it from this perspective, your mindset literally defines your future. You are constantly co-creating your reality with the greater forces in the universe, and the secret to a deeply enriching experience of life is buried between your ears and inside your heart: your inner world. Your dreams, your goals, your wealth, your health, your relationships – they all depend on it.

If we empower our psychology, we can manifest a future for ourselves that is far more inspiring, bigger, and brighter than anything we dared dream of growing up. And if we don't master our mindset, our attitude, our relationship with ourselves and life? Then the chances are that our limitations will get the better of us and we *will* die with the music still inside us. Is that not a price too great to pay and a cost too heavy to bear?

So now, it's time to discover the one, two, or many 'issues' that have become a burden to achieving your dreams so that you can dissolve them. Let's dive deep into your psyche and shine the light on your fears, worries, and concerns. Let's release you from the often-self-imposed limitations and restrictions that cause you to feel trapped or stuck. Let's set you free so you can live the life you were born for. That is what I would love for you, above all else.

If you are asking yourself why some people fulfil their dreams while you seem to struggle, this book is for you. If many years of your time here have passed and you feel that you haven't made the most of it yet, you are in the right place. And if you have had enough of living small, being lost, or feeling unfulfilled, then welcome, because I wrote this book to help you overcome exactly that. Together, we will explore the invisible, mental, spiritual, and emotional limits that cause you to hold back in life so you can go beyond them. This is my dedication to you, and it is what this journey is all about.

May this book bring you the insight you need to reach new heights in your life. May it help you understand what bothers you and break through it. May it give you new ideas for new ways to master your future. And may it inspire you to fulfil your dreams… because that is what you were born for.

Here's to your life without limits.

1
DREAMING SMALL

"The future belongs to those who believe in the beauty of their dreams."

ELEANOR ROOSEVELT

It is entirely possible that you have gone through your whole life without realising that you have extraordinary potential within you. That you have spent your years believing that you are ordinary, small, insignificant, or powerless. Or that despite inherently sensing that you can be, do, become, achieve, and experience so much more, you have been told the opposite. Perhaps you believe that you are nothing special, that life is hard, that you must work, work, work, and that you must fulfil your obligations, doing what is 'right' rather than what inspires your heart.

Maybe you have spent too much time listening to the nay-sayers or believing all of the reasons that you think you can't do *more* with your life and now your heartfelt dreams seem crushed under the weight of small expectations, logical explanations, irrational fears, and limiting opinions. Or maybe you have been holding back from your higher calling out of fear that what you desire won't happen for you. Essentially, you have almost stopped believing that great things *can* happen for you.

Well, I am here to be the voice of inspiration that you need. In the midst of your struggle, doubts, and disbelief, I am here to let you know that there is a bigger life out there for you. In the midst of your pain and suffering, I am here to tell you that this world has far more in store for you than you imagine right now. I am here to let you know that yes, you can start from exactly where you are and create your dream life, one step, one day, one leap of faith, and one act of courage at a time. It is not your destiny to shrink and suffer. It is your destiny to RISE and THRIVE.

It is your *destiny* to find your purpose here; the purpose you were born with and the one that you yearn to fulfil. You are phenomenally gifted with talents and skills and knowledge and wisdom inside you, and you *can* turn your calling into a career, impact thousands of people, become known around the world, earn your fortune, and illuminate the lives of many. You can discover your dharma, unleash your power, and claim your unique and meaningful place on the stage of life.

There are far greater possibilities available in this life, and they are available for YOU. You can own a business, run companies, run races, initiate movements, design your future, live outside the box, travel the globe, create waves in the world. We can do *so* much with what we have been given, and sometimes we just need an outside influence to remind us that we weren't born for an ordinary life. Sometimes that is all it takes to ignite the spark within us and give us the hope and determination we need to pursue the path we *really* want for ourselves.

When I was just 20 years old and still finding my way through depression, I was living in a townhouse in Bulimba, Brisbane. One night, I was sitting on the curb outside my home at around 9:00pm.

Looking down at the road, I was feeling particularly lost. I wondered how I would ever move forwards with my life, let alone create one that I loved. My despair was overwhelming… and then divine intervention occurred.

Suddenly, I lifted my head and saw an older gentleman walking up the hill towards me. He was well-dressed, wearing a suit, and walking with a cane. As he walked closer to me, I considered returning inside as I was visibly upset, but my intuition told me to stay exactly where I was. The gentleman approached and then stopped beside me. He asked me if I was okay, in that special way that strips you raw and has you feel completely seen, heard, felt, and cared for.

Then he said this to me: "I've had an amazing life. I've travelled, run businesses, and met people everywhere. There is a big world out there for you." He spoke with such deep certainty, wisdom, grace, and love that his words touched my core. The truth of his message resonated deeply inside my heart.

I knew then that the moment of struggle and angst I was experiencing didn't have to last forever and that I could get beyond it. Glimpses of how I wanted my future to be flashed through my mind. My spirit lifted and a surge of hope washed over me. That one man's words inspired me to commit to my calling, to overcome my depression, and to take a full-bodied leap into the future I dreamed of – and he will forever live in my heart because of his presence in my life that day.

We are all capable of achieving and experiencing inspiring things – just look at what people are doing in the world around you to prove that to yourself. Your time here on Earth does *not* have to be a continuous journey of difficulty, filled with years of suffering and sadness. There is far, far more to life than paying bills until you die. Life is a precious chance for so, so much more than this. You know it in your bones, you know it in your heart, and you know it in your soul.

You know that you were born for meaningful pursuits, audacious goals, heart-filled projects, purposeful causes, great legacies, and incredible accomplishments. This is not a fantasy or a wishy-washy notion: it's a fact. We are made of the same potential as the entire universe – the same force that created our world and everything in it also created *you*. This is not a small thing, and the honourable way to celebrate that magnificence that breathed life into you is to create a life that is truly worthy of you; one that mirrors the very essence of who you were born to be.

So, just in case you have never been told or just in case you need to hear it again: you are EXTRAORDINARY. And just in case no one has ever said it to you lately: you CAN do great things with your life. And just in case anyone has made you believe otherwise: you DESERVE MORE. And just in case you feel like no one has noticed your potential: I SEE you. Own it. Embrace it. Pursue it. Achieve it. Because YOU were born for more.

2
AIMLESS LIVING

"People get to where they want to go because they know where they want to go. Most people are driven by what they think they should do. The most important question you can ask yourself is 'What do I really want?' Once you can establish that answer for yourself, have every thing you do and every choice you make move you in the direction of your vision."

OPRAH WINFREY

Every single moment, minute, hour, and day of your life is a chance to follow your inspiration, to express yourself fully, to achieve great things, and to grow into exactly the person you are destined to be. Every moment that you breathe is a gift. Your existence is a gift. Your time here is a gift. Your life is a gift. Are you crystal clear on what you would love to do with it?

Not knowing who we are, what we want, or why we are here holds our potential back. These are all incredibly important keys to a life of meaning and yet so many people struggle with defining their destiny. They feel confronted with the blank canvas of their own future, and they have no idea where to start in blueprinting and building a life that is full of depth, profundity, energy, and inspiration. It is no wonder that depression and mental illnesses are common globally: so many are living aimlessly.

Living aimlessly is typically caused by three things: disconnection from one's purpose, clouded dreams, and an absence of meaningful goals… and your purpose is the key to unlocking it all. What is 'it'? *It* is a life that lights you up; the one that moves you from within; the one you love to wake up to; the one you have to pinch yourself to believe; the one where you feel deeply blessed.

Without question, lacking a sense of purpose, suppressing my dreams, and having no goals was the primary cause of the near-suicidal depression I experienced in my late teenage years. I had no vision for my immediate future, and I felt so lost that I considered ending it all. But when I reconnected with my purpose, committed to my dreams, and started setting goals again, it saved my life. They were what turned *everything* around for me; the clarity on what I *truly* wanted to do that set a new and meaningful future in motion, one that I thank myself and God for every single day.

When you haven't yet discovered your soulful purpose on Earth, you tend to feel disconnected, depressed, and lost. You lack the intuitive sense of direction that automatically appears when you find out what you love to do. Life seems to lack meaning because you haven't discovered the meaning of your life yet. Days, weeks, months, and years go by while you quietly wonder what it is all for. You yearn for something greater under the surface, knowing you were born for something more.

Your purpose is your true north. It is your compass to navigate your way through life. It illuminates you – and your life – from within. The spark of what you were born to do ignites your dreams. It sparks your what (*what* you would love to do with your life) and why (*why* this is meaningful for you). It gives you *vision* for life: a moving picture inside your mind and heart of the type of life you would love to experience and what you would love to achieve.

When you aren't 'plugged in' to your purpose, you either dream small or you don't dream at all. Instead of shooting for the stars, you accept the relationships, the job, the wealth, the health that show up on your path without questioning whether this life, the one you are living, is the one that inspires you. You never ask for or aim for more, and so your life feels more ordinary than extraordinary. The heartbreaking reality is that because they are disconnected from their calling, so many people do die with the music still inside them, with unfulfilled dreams inside their heart.

Once your vision comes into focus, you can then set meaningful goals for your life. These are goals that touch you, that unleash determination from within you, that you can't wait to work on, and that you can't wait to achieve. It is this singleness of vision that can guide our entire journey here, but only if we surrender to it and trust it to lead us to awe-inspiring and remarkable places.

We NEED our purpose, dreams, and goals to inspire us; to make plans; to tap into our gifts; to thrive. Without aspirations that move us to rise up, we float. We flail. We fall. Adversities become increasingly difficult to overcome because we can't see what is or could be on the other side of the hurdles we face. Our wounds defeat us, drama drains us, and our obstacles get the better of us.

Our life feels colourless, empty, flat, and, yes, purposeless. But *with* purpose, *with* dreams, *with* goals, you will ignite your life from deep within. Your zest for life will return. You will find your fire and determination. *You* will come to life.

Perhaps you have lost touch with what you are here to do. Perhaps it has been years since you dreamed about greater possibilities. Or perhaps you haven't set your goals because you aren't sure what you want yet. Regardless of why you have been feeling flat, take the time and make the effort to get clear on who you are and what you want. Look inside your heart. Remember your dharma. Find out what you would love to devote your life to. Set milestones that, as you achieve them, will let you know that you are living the life you promised yourself.

No matter how long it takes, even if it takes a year, give this gift to yourself. Find your purpose, discover your dreams, and set your goals, so you can spend less time wondering what you are here for and more time fulfilling your aspirations. Trust me: it is within you, the astounding and life-transforming clarity about how you would love to spend your limited window of time here. Admit it to yourself. Reveal it. Release it from the depths of your own heart so that you can say goodbye to emptiness and hello to a life filled with magic.

I don't know where I would be today if I hadn't discovered my purpose, unleashed my dreams, and pursued my goals – and I don't know where YOUR purpose, dreams, and goals will take you in the future. But what I do know is that they *are* the key to a life you love, a life that brings out the best of you and gives you the best of everything, and that they are worth searching for.

3
UNDERESTIMATING YOURSELF

"You were designed for accomplishment, engineered for success, and endowed with the seeds of greatness."

ZIG ZIGLAR

The heartbreaking truth is that so many people believe that they have little or no value. On a painfully personal level, they feel that they are somehow worthless or undeserving of a great life. They have no idea just how beautiful, original, funny, smart, clever, sassy, wise, and profound they are. How valued. How loved. How cared for. How needed. How appreciated. They feel small, and so they shrink themselves further, hiding in the shadows of a life that feels empty.

Maybe you can relate. Maybe you, too, have settled for a life that is less than you desire because you feel deep down that you are just ordinary. Maybe you have been putting yourself last, sideling your goals and dreams, and deprioritising your wants and needs. Maybe you are so busy shining the light on others that you haven't discovered why you are worthy of the spotlight, too. If this rings true for you, I am here to let you know that *just by being who you are*, you light up the world around you.

The truth is that you are extraordinary – no exception. You are simply not owning your innate value. Your gifts. Your talents. Your skills.

Your knowledge. Your experience. Your wisdom. Your mastery. Your genius. You haven't studied yourself closely enough to discover your unique expression of that extraordinary essence we are all made of. You haven't explored the depths of who you are yet.

Instead, you have probably spent far too much time living inside a story that you are average. You might assume that you have nothing much to share with the world. Or you might believe that others were born with far greater abilities or talents than you. Maybe you have experienced a series of failures, adversities, or struggles and you have lost touch with your remarkable nature as a result. Or perhaps you are judging yourself so harshly that you can't see the truth of how phenomenal you are and therefore, you have decided you are not 'one of the special ones' born and destined to succeed.

Whatever your inner feeling or belief about yourself may be, it's time to break the story and write a new one: a story where you are the hero, the champion, the legend, not the sidekick nor the extra in the movie of your life. A story where you win. Feel alive. Thrive. Glisten. Radiate. Receive. You have sold yourself short – believe me – and that inner story you tell yourself about who you are, what you do or do not believe you are capable and worthy of colours everything.

You might think, "Oh, I couldn't do that" or "Others succeed, but not me" or "I don't have much to offer." This then defines your entire future: your future actions, your future feelings, your future achievements, results, track record, meaning, and fulfilment. You believe you are missing the X factor that your heroes seem to have, when, actually, it is and has always been within you.

Being too shy to acknowledge and appreciate your gifts and your greatness undermines your dreams, shrinks your goals, and cuts your purpose off at the knees. When we think we are small, we play small. When we feel small, we aim small. This is why it is essential to expand our perception of ourselves to see *all* of who we are, not just what we see on the surface. It is why opening our mind and our heart to see our giftedness matters. It is why a healthy and objective appreciation of our strengths is crucial. It is why *loving* ourselves wholly counts greatly.

You came into this world with the seeds of your gifts within you and the spark of potential within you. It is still there today, as you sit there reading this. It never dies. Your life is a stage to be who you are, and you are being guided to do exactly that: to use what is within you, to do what you love and what you want to do, and to be who you want to be... because *that* is how you unlock your raw potential and touch the world. It is how you live an inspired life.

Struggling with confidence? As you express and share your gifts, you will find it. Wondering if you are worthy? As you experience the powerful difference that you can make on the lives of those around you: your family, friends, clients, customers, fans, followers, even total strangers, you will discover your innate value. As you move down your path taking one courageous step at a time, you will get to know the *real* you, the inspiring being that you are.

When this time comes, it will be impossible to question your worth because there is simply too much evidence to the contrary. I want you to reach this point in your life: where you *know* how infinitely precious you are, where you know your path and place here, and where you are living boldly and fully and wholly and allowing life to bless you every single day and in so, so many ways, with all the miracles and opportunities meant perfectly for you.

You have no idea just how much you are capable of. But you will never discover it if you keep taking yourself at surface value and holding back from the life and the career you were born for. As long as you keep shrinking yourself, you will shrink your life and sacrifice what matters the most to you.

It is not arrogant to recognise your worth, to acknowledge your value, to discover and own your gifts, to claim your power. It is necessary. It is healthy. It is inspiring. Why? Because then you will get out of your own way and let your entire life flourish, from your health to your career to your relationships and your bank accounts. Because then you will spend less time beating yourself up and more time doing your thing in the world, *for* this world. Because then we can all benefit from the phenomenal and imperfectly perfect human being that you are. You deserve so much. Never forget that.

4
SUCCESS GUILT

"One can never consent to creep when one feels an impulse to soar."
HELEN KELLER

It's time to address success guilt. What is success guilt? It is the notion that when you hit it big in your career, life, and wealth, it will trigger people. It is the assumption that your outrageous success will cause pain for others: that they will feel small, insignificant, or ordinary when YOU shine. Essentially, you worry that people will feel bitter or envious as you rise into the small percentage of humanity who *love* their lives.

Your success guilt could be directed towards your partner, your social circles, your social media followers, or even your clients. You might feel resistant to the idea of outearning your family ten times over or be fearful that people will misunderstand you, judge you, or disown you as you excel.

Or you might wonder, "Who am I to thrive while millions are living in poverty?" And so, you play it small. In some cases, far, far smaller than you dream of. Instead of standing out, you hide out. Instead of rising up, you hold back. You pretend that you don't want for much when the exact opposite is true.

If this resonates and you *know* that success guilt is causing you to work hard but avoid the big break – *your* big break – that would skyrocket you into the stratosphere, ask yourself this: where does the idea that you succeeding is a 'bad' thing come from? Does it stem from an experience where you outshone someone you care about; a friend, a sibling, a colleague? Did someone express envy or resentment in a moment when you excelled?

Discover the source of your success guilt. Identify where your assumption came from, that it is somehow your job to make everyone succeed together. It means getting to the heart of why you feel uncomfortable doing or having 'more' than others. And once you know where it stems from, work on overturning the feeling that it is selfish to pursue your dreams or that it serves the world more somehow if you achieve only a mediocre level of success.

Many years ago, a friend from high school said to me, "You got all of the good life." The tone of his comment was pure envy, and it almost triggered a wave of success guilt. But then I remembered the tens of thousands of dollars I had invested into my personal growth, how many hours of deep healing work I had done, the courage it took for me to pursue an original path, and how hard I had worked to create my authentic life... and my guilt dissolved in an instant.

That is the ultimate antidote to success guilt: remembering that you have, in all probability, fought extremely hard to be where you are today. It is to reflect on just how far you have come, the determination it took to heal your body or grow a career or attract the right partner, and to never forget that it didn't always come easy. In fact, it's possible that it was the hardest thing you have ever done.

It puts the idea of feeling guilty for your achievements into harsh perspective when you remember the sleepless nights, the down days, the doubts, and the meltdowns you endured along the way. You CHOSE this – to do whatever it took to achieve this – and you worked for it. You harnessed your willpower to keep going when it got tough and to do what others were not willing to do so that you can experience a life that few do. Don't ever apologise for that.

Success guilt is the idea that when you stand in the light, you will cast a shadow over someone else. But you must remember two things. The first is that people can *choose* to stand in your shadow, or they can choose to stand beside you. The second is that by you shining, you illuminate the path for others. Yes, it might challenge them in the interim – by confronting their current lack of fulfilment – but it will help them by showing them what is possible and offering them the opportunity to decide if they also want more from their life.

While I honour with my whole heart your desire for others to rise with you, you cannot make them do it. It is impossible. You can empower them, yes. You can be an example, yes. You can inspire them, yes. You can share the wisdom you have gained along the way, yes. Yet, try as you might, you can lead a horse to water, but you cannot make it drink.

The idea that doing well for yourself is painful for others stems from a scarcity mindset. It assumes that, as you succeed, you will take something away from someone else, or that there aren't enough riches and accomplishments in this world for all of us – when this is far from the truth. Therefore, it is vital to acknowledge that we live in an extraordinary universe on an extraordinary planet in an extraordinary time in history AND that each person has the chance to make something of their life. But it is up to them to do so. That is not on you.

We *all* have the potential to be more, do more, and go to great places. It's just that you allowed yourself to do it. You loved yourself enough to make the most of the time you have. And now, as you continue to rise, you can be an example that this world needs – an example of someone who beat the odds and *made it*. An example of someone who transcended their pain to find and forge a new way forward.

We each have unique gifts to share, and we must realise that there is enough opportunity and prosperity in this world for all of us, that there *is* room at the top for all those driven enough to reach for it. To believe anything else will shortcut our experience of life, triggering success guilt and causing us to feel bitter and envious when *we* see other people skyrocketing on their path because *we* haven't given ourselves permission to thrive.

My final note on success guilt is this: as you do rise (because you will) and as others are triggered by it (because, inevitably, some people will be), have the courage to stand in the face of their wounding and be greater. Rise above it. Then seek to ignite others. To inspire them. Light the path. Pass the torch. Share your experience. Let your life unlock a brighter future for humanity. This is your time, and you have *earned* it.

5
Spiritual Separation

"There is a divine presence, a divine order, in the universe that few people ever get to know, but those who do, their lives are changed forever."

Dr John Demartini, paraphrasing Leibniz

Do you believe with certainty that there is a plan for your life? That you were born with a purpose and that you are being guided to fulfil it? That you are never on your own in this universe, even when it feels like you are? That things *do* happen for an often unrecognised but important reason? Or do you believe that you are separate from everything and everyone around you? That there is no hidden intelligence and higher plan to life?

My experience is that people who feel there is a divine order to the world we live in tend to go further and experience deeper meaning than those who believe that there is no rhyme or reason to the events we encounter. They allow God to be the air beneath their wings, picking them up when they are down, and supporting them to travel to great places. Instead of struggling with every little thing, they surrender. Instead of fighting the flow, they flow with life. Instead of feeling weak, they allow the spirit within them and the spirit beyond them to provide them with strength for their journey.

At the very least, those who believe in a higher power tend to have a life that is filled with heart-opening awe and personal growth. Why? Because in acknowledging that there is something far greater than us at work beyond us, we realise that things do happen for a reason and it is, in fact, not entirely upon us to do it all or do it all ourselves.

We realise that our darkest hours often give rise to our greatest accomplishments and that our greatest tragedies can give rise to our greatest triumphs and therefore, there is a higher plan to our life here. We experience synchronicities and divine interference often. We feel seen, heard, guided, and *loved* by the force that created us.

What is the divine order? It is the invisible omnipotent force that created us, everyone, and everything we have ever known. It is the infinite potential that resides at your core. It is the universal intelligence that permeates every aspect and every moment of our existence. It is the deep sense within us of what we are born to do, of what is the 'right' way to go in our life. It is the place where all intuitions, synchronicities, manifestations, ideas, and confirmations come from. It is the silent but potent power that we are touched and moved by every single day.

Discovering the higher order and a greater plan for life doesn't mean that you will spend your time sitting on a meditation pillow praying for all your problems to be solved without also taking bold and continuous action. It means forming a powerful partnership with the force that is beyond you – call it God, the divine plan, the higher intelligence, the ether, the universe – to co-create *magic* in your life, your career, your relationships, your body, your wealth, and the world.

It means following your inspiration, your intuition, and your path of purpose and walking in lockstep with the divine as it opens doors and draws miracles and opportunities onto your path; the right relationships, ideas, solutions, and signs at just the right moment. It means allowing yourself to be humbled by the beauty, perfection, and love of the world around you and letting it inspire the world within you.

When you feel as though you are flying blind, you know the divine will guide the way… and when it does? You will feel compelled to follow the path, to leap into action, to do what you have been guided to do. As you open your heart and mind to the heavens, your life will feel far less like a game of chance or a random series of challenging situations and more like a miraculous story unfolding. Instead of being fearful of the future and hardened by your circumstances, you will approach life with extraordinary trust: trust in yourself and in the perfection that surrounds you.

Thinking that we are here to suffer only slows and weighs us down, and believing that life is working against us causes us to attract that exact experience: struggle. Yes, you will be challenged, tested, trialled on your path. It is an unavoidable part of becoming who we are capable of being and doing what we are capable of doing. But suffering in those challenges is a choice.

You can choose to resist every seemingly difficult experience – or you can lean in and let it grow you. You can fight against the very rhythms and currents of life – or you can find healing by going with the flow. You can tell yourself that life has no meaning – or you can find the meaning of *yours*. You can keep believing you are alone or that your life is an endless battle – or you can connect with the higher intelligence and let life guide your path.

You don't have to figure it all out yourself, suffer for longer than is necessary, live a life filled with adversity, be lost forever, or feel depressed every day. You can find your way forwards, taking your inspiring place in the world and living a life overflowing with moving experiences.

It is not all on your shoulders, and nor does it have to be. If you recognise that you are also a manifestation of a higher power and thus your entire life is an expression of it, it will set your future on a new trajectory. When you express curiosity, gratitude, and humility for the universe we live in, endless creative possibilities, opportunities, pathways, and solutions will appear for you.

Although it may feel like it at times, the purpose of your life is not for you to suffer – it is for you to fulfil *your* purpose – and when you recognise this, you will start to rise. When we realise that we all belong here, that we do have potential, and that we were and have been designed to excel, we become ignited from within. When we surrender our human stuff and find love in our pain, we become lighter. When we let ourselves be nudged, called, pushed, and pulled forward to our destiny, life becomes a tear-jerking adventure.

No more believing that you are alone in this world. No more believing that you aren't seen, heard, or felt in this life. No more thinking you are separate from everything around you or that you have been somehow forgotten or missed by the divine. You were created with purpose and with a purpose in mind. Life is on your side. Recognise it and RISE.

6
Family Imprints

"Don't be peer pressured into being less than you are."
Dr Steve Maraboli

What is accepted to be 'normal' by our family: who we are expected to be, what we are expected to do, or what our parents either believe or believed is possible and appropriate in life. All of these family imprints can shape, enable, encourage, or limit what we feel is possible for ourselves and, therefore, how our life pans out.

You need your family. Of course, you do. You wouldn't be here without them. But where family imprints become a limit to your greater potential – what you yearn for, for yourself and your life – is when what you dream of conflicts with what your family accepts and expects. It is when what you feel called to do goes against what you were raised to do.

You want riches, but your parents felt uncomfortable with flashy displays of wealth, believing that the rich are greedy. You want to touch millions of lives, but your mother or father preached against being famous, claiming that to be in the spotlight is vain. You want to earn exceptionally well in your career, but your grandparents believed in 'work hard, don't ask for more' and lived their entire lives with just enough money to get by.

You want to break out of a religion, start a spiritual movement, change a generational pattern, stand out from the crowd, have ten kids or no kids, marry once, marry three times, launch a company, be the boss, write controversial content, sing on stage, blaze your own trail, be bold, be powerful, be innovative, create a revolution, leave a global legacy.

But ask yourself this: is there anything in your aspirations for the future that doesn't sit comfortably with how you were brought up? Which family constructs, idealisms, morals, beliefs, or strong-held ideas are you challenging simply by pursuing what *you* feel born to do? Is what you dream of doing simply not how things were 'done' when you were young?

Take a moment now and look within. What kind of life do or did your parents expect you to have? Did you choose your current career path for yourself or for your family? Do you feel that you need your parents' approval for life decisions, even if you are now an adult? Where does the inner pressure to succeed come from? Are you doing what you truly love or following in the footsteps of your parents because you think you ought to? Are you deeply congruent with what you want to achieve in this world? Do you feel free on every level to be who you are?

Your family is your first tribe. In most cases, you wouldn't have survived without them. They provided a source of belonging, comfort, wellbeing, advice, and examples on what to do (or not do) in life. And so, it might require courage – immense courage, in fact – to break away from this often deeply ingrained family mould and write a new story for yourself.

It will take courage to imagine the type of life *you* would love, irrespective of your background. To decide that what you want is not just a dream, it is your DESTINY, regardless of whether your family understands. And then, to forge your way forwards, despite critical opinions from your loved ones. To give the highest service of love to yourself and to your soul, first and foremost.

That is the opportunity you have in your life today: to take the strengths, the gifts, and the beautiful qualities your family instilled within you – whether that is determination in the face of extreme adversity or the power of generosity or creativity or deep love – and bring them forwards with you, the way *you* dream.

You do not necessarily have less or more of an advantage in life because of the family you grew up with or because of who your parents are or were. Your life is the result of how you choose to write your own story. And because of this, it is crucial when unlocking our potential to refrain from blaming any parent, sibling, or career for 'the way we are'. Who we were raised to be and what kind of life we were raised to live only limits us from the life we dream of if we allow it. The buck stops with us.

Decide now: what ripple do you want to set in motion for the generations after you? What would you love to ignite in people because of the way you choose to live and what you do in your lifetime? What message do you want to share with humanity? What will you do with this gift of life, this precious and finite moment on Earth, that your family, your parents, gave you?

We cannot control nor can we change the kind of childhood we had, what our parents did, the imprints from their generation or the generations before them. It is done. It is part of your history now. But what we can do is decide how we will raise *ourselves* from this moment onwards. We can decide how we will bring out our strengths and what we will do with our abilities. We can make up our own mind about the world around us, what we feel we are capable of, what our plans for the future are. We can chart our course to the horizon and beyond.

It IS your life, after all. Your life. No one else's. You are property of the universe, not of your parents or any other family member – nor anyone else for that matter. You are a sovereign being with a destiny to fulfil. So, be the one who writes the story and creates the future. Show up for yourself. Commit to creating an extraordinary life.

And then remember that achieving outrageous success by doing what you love, by sharing your heartfelt God-given gifts with humanity *is* the greatest way to honour your parents and your entire family lineage. Why? Because it shows them that they raised an original leader. A genius. A huge heart. A human with a mission and a fire burning so bright inside them that nothing can stop them from the life of their dreams. That is love.

7
Uninspiring Influences

"If you look at the people in your circle and you don't get inspired, then you don't have a circle. You have a cage."

Nipsey Hussle

Although it has been said before, it absolutely must be said again: you become who you hang out with. Humans are social creatures and so it is natural that we will want to spend our life with people in our personal circles, our social circles, our community circles, and our work circles. We engage with humanity throughout the many years of our life by interacting with those who surround us.

What we must be mindful of, however, is the truth that whether we like it or not, we *are* influenced by the people we spend time with. The influence may be subtle, and it might even take years to occur, but we do make an imprint on each other. We meet minds, have conversations, exchange ideas, develop behaviours together, and absorb one another's energy. We shape and are shaped by those we connect with on our path.

This is why we must realise that we are always risking becoming exactly that which we spend our time with. If your inner circle is full of people who have heavy energy, who don't care enough to aspire for more, or who simply bring your mood down through their attitudes, you end up swimming against the current when trying to unleash your own potential in life.

One of the greatest blessings of my life is that I began associating with entrepreneurs from as early as 18 years old. Right out of the gate, I was spending my time with and was influenced by people who believed in possibility. People who had founded companies and launched national projects and global movements. People who had risen to leadership in all types of industries, from the environment to economic charities. People who were changing the world, running businesses, and running their own destiny.

These people *inspired me*. They showed me new ways of living, setting an example by aligning their heart with their work and growing enterprises that made a difference. They invited me to consider possibilities for my life that were far greater than what I knew existed when I was still in school.

This is a gift: when the people you spend time with not only light up a different, brighter path in front of you, but they light you up from within. Where they see who YOU are. When they recognise the spark within you and encourage it to burn, baby, burn. We *need* these people in our lives to push us to greater pastures and to remind us of who we are in trying times when it seems like we might never make it. They mirror our heart, spirit, and potential back to us.

Today, I am certain that my achievements and dreams have largely been made possible because of those social circles I established early on in my journey. In fact, I remember the moment a contact Philip Krieg rang me when I was age 19, working a shift in retail selling books, and asked me, "Did you know you can get paid to write?" That *one* conversation with the right person at the right time literally changed my destiny forever and led to the life I have now. Where would I be without those extraordinary people?

Make a careful assessment of the people you associate with most. Who do you share your precious time, space, and life with on a daily or weekly basis? Are your social circles expansive? Are they big thinkers? Original thinkers? Creatives? Are the conversations inspiring or depressing? Are your closest friends going places?

Or are they cruising in a job without any end goal in mind? Are they making waves or trying to ride someone else's? Do they feel like a victim of what happens 'to them' or do they look deeper to discover truth, refusing to let the challenging events of their life become the story of their life?

In my humble opinion, it is exponentially more rewarding to spend time alone in contemplation, journaling, healing work, reading, rejuvenation, walking, and studying than to be engaged in social dynamics that drain you. You have a purpose to fulfil and drama, gossip, complaining, blaming, and politics can undermine your goals. You can't afford this. Your time and energy are precious, and the people in your life are either going to slow you down from achieving your dreams or help you accelerate towards them (and yes, this applies to family and intimate relationships, too).

Your dreams can be ignited or extinguished, fuelled or crushed, encouraged or diminished by the people you spend time with. So, be conscious of your contacts and relationships. All you need is just one person who *sees* you and *believes* in you to ignite a prosperous and purposeful change in your life. Make an effort to spend time with people with whom you are unfiltered, raw, real, untamed, wild, free, deep, profound.

The crazy ones who GET you. Those who SEE you. Those who feel you even when you're not around, who know you are down before you do, and who will throw you a lifeline when you need it. The people who inspire you, move you, heal you, and touch you. Those with whom you require no labels, no masks, no façades, no explanation, nor justification. Seek them out.

They will reflect your magnificence back to you so you can see it in critical moments. They will infuse your life with greatness, with vigour, with new ideas, with refreshing perspectives, and encouragement: the stuff that dreams are made of. You need this if you are to turn your life around, start out on a new path, elevate your success, and influence the world.

Here's a tip from my soul brother and talented stuntman, Bálint Józsa: if you don't have this type of person in your immediate environment, read their books instead. Browse their videos on YouTube. Listen to their podcasts. Attend their seminars. Follow, listen to, and learn from the greatest leaders of all time, the people who achieved great feats and shifted industries and made history. Find a way to be amongst them and allow their light to ignite yours. Allow their presence to shift the way you see yourself and awaken new potential in your life.

People like this – the dreamers, the risk-takers, the leaders, the visionaries, the entrepreneurs, the healers – are worth their weight in gold, and the future you dream of may depend on their very presence. I know mine did. So, fill your life with *only* the type of person who is focused on what matters, who lives out their purpose, and who gives others permission to play a bigger game… because then, very soon, you will become one of those people for the world.

8
Following The Crowd

"Don't let the fear of what other people think hold you back. You're not going to give an account to people of what you did with your life. You're going to give an account to God."

Joel Osteen

To fulfil our potential, to reach for our greatness, to express all that we are, and to achieve what is possible for us, we must live a life that is guided by our heart and soul. Why? Because it is only when we connect with and tune in to what inspires and ignites us that we can live a deeply authentic life – and seldom can we do this when we are following the crowd.

The life of greatness and meaning that you yearn for requires you to live from the inside-out, not from the outside-in. When we live from the outside-in, we listen to social norms and try to follow them. We care more about what other people think than what we think. We dilute our authenticity to fit in. We worry endlessly about whether we will be liked, accepted, or approved of. We suppress what we feel called to do because it is 'different' from what 'everyone else' is doing.

As a result, we end up living a cookie-cutter life. While who we are and what we do might look good or make sense to the outside world, it costs us greatly as this disconnection with our own spirit, our own uniqueness, leaves us feeling empty. It is because of this that harnessing our courage to shift from an externally driven life to a life directed by the soul, by our transcendent self, is worth every effort.

When we live our life from the inside-out, we choose the lifestyle, the career path, the work-life, the family, and personal life we love, and we do what it takes to manifest that. We find and pursue what lights us up, what moves us, what fulfils us. We become more interested in how aligned our own life is with our heart, our soul, and our dream for the future than whether it looks impressive to the outside.

An original and authentic life is filled with meaning, purpose, depth, and your own perfect expression of success. To fulfil this, we must surrender the masks we live behind, the faces we put on, the façades we try to show the world, even the roles we have been playing. The cost is real, but the reward is immense… because now, you are *free*. Free to move in this world and to live the life you were born for.

Trying to fit in or hide who we are won't work for long and sacrificing what you yearn for in your soul isn't sustainable. If you are living out of alignment with who you are, you will eventually be led back to your heart – the truth of who you are and what you love to do. And this is what we crave: a life where we can be ourselves. If we are not being ourselves, how can we fulfil ourselves? How can we be loved for who we are? How can we carve out or find a career we love with our whole heart if we are hiding our heart, trying to follow the masses?

Is the race you are running your own? The push for success. Why? What's it for? The drive to do more. Where does it come from? Who you think you are meant to be. What created that idea? Are you living a life you don't love because you think that is the norm? Or because the people around you live that way? Are you spending your valuable energy and using up your mental-emotional bandwidth trying to be 'enough' or 'just right'? Is the path you are on the one you *want* to be on? What do YOU want to achieve? This self-reflection is essential if we are to live a life of wonder and meaning.

There are unique keys to your fulfilment in this life, essential building blocks that make your life feel extraordinary when they are present. Knowing yours is the starting point of the future that inspires you. My keys to fulfilment are writing, self-development, career, travel (city lights are my favourite), speaking, and mentoring. When I fill my life with these, I thrive. The same applies to you. To live *your* life, clarify your building blocks, the keys to *your* fulfilment, and then build your life around them.

Rather than filling your entire life with what you think you should do or trying to be who others want you to be, live from your own heart, regardless of outer opinion, pressure, or expectation. Live in such deep alignment with your soul that you do what you do simply because it feels 'right' in your core, not because it looks shiny and perfect to watchful eyes.

You are not here to impress people; you are here to inspire people. You are not here to be loved by everyone; you are here to share your love with people. You are not here to be the best; you are here to be *your* best. You are here for a unique life with accomplishments, experiences, an approach to living, perspectives, philosophies, work, connections, and creativity that feel special to YOU, not to the world around you.

That desire for an authentic life burns strong within you. You want a life unedited by others perspectives; away from their crushing opinions or heavy ideas about what you are meant to do, could do, or ought to do in order to be valuable, worthy, or acceptable. The flame never goes out because you are here to be YOU. To follow YOUR path. To go your own way. To set trends, do what you feel in your heart, let your truth out, use your unique gifts, and be fulfilled on every level.

So, shed the expectations that have been projected onto you and set yourself free. Why? Because the biggest regret you could have in your life is to spend the infinitely precious and limited years of your time here with your ladder up the wrong wall trying to live a life that is not your own.

Trying to compete. To measure up. To fit in. To stifle your character. To belong at the cost of your own peace. To work hard on something that doesn't matter in the end. To give up *your* limited window of life on Earth to do what simply doesn't call out to or inspire you. You deserve more – and you know it.

9
Comparison Obsession

"Comparison is the crush of conformity from one side and competition from the other. It's trying to simultaneously fit in and stand out."

Brené Brown

Comparison obsession is the persistent habit of measuring yourself against other people to firstly, see how well you are doing (a progress check), and secondly, assess your power and value. It is the pattern of using others and the way they live and what they do as a measuring stick for *your* success and thus, your worth, because the two are so often inherently connected in our minds.

Here's what happens when we endlessly compare ourselves to others: we invalidate, judge, rank, or minimise ourselves in comparison. We do this with our mentors, our parents, our teachers, our leaders; the celebrities, athletes, and entrepreneurs of the world; or even with our closest friends. We see someone's outstanding results and instead of simply appreciating their expression of human greatness, we knock ourselves down thinking that we must 'suck'.

In doing this, we distract ourselves from producing our original work, assuming that our gifts are inferior and that there isn't enough room or a need in the world for what *we* can do. We delay doing what we feel called to. We put off doing the necessary apprenticeship to perfect our craft and develop mastery.

We become so busy peeking over the fence at other people's yards and picking ourselves apart that we never build the life we dream of. Instead of seeing our legends as inspiration, we stand in their shadows and hide from our own potent, luminescent light, casting darkness over our own life. The impact of this is detrimental and far-reaching.

The other side of the comparison coin is where we think we are somehow ahead of or better than other people. Although we might not say it outwardly, we may silently criticise the people around us, judging their life choices, thinking that we are winning, or that we are superior in some way. We puff ourselves up, become a little arrogant, and can start to preach our way of life, our strategy, our truth, as *the* one to follow to the exclusion of all others.

I've done it; you've done it; we've all done it at times. All I'll say about this one is this: if you need to boost your self-esteem by looking down on those whom you think have done less or achieved less than you, then you are not at peace with yourself. It merely indicates that there is some wounding or weakness lurking under the surface, crying out for healing. Work on it. Come back into your heart. Tend to *your* path. Turn your attention back to your own life and make moves on your next feat, instead of wasting your energy judging other people's lives.

Perhaps the obsession of comparing ourselves to those around us starts in childhood where we try to win or be bigger or better than our siblings, assessing our place in the family or competing for our parents' attention. Or maybe we develop it during our schooling years where we are assessed and categorised based on our various levels of ability, genius, talent, and charisma. Or perhaps it goes back even further than that, to past times when we had to find our place in the tribe if we were to survive.

But no matter where it stems from or why we are so inclined to measure ourselves and our results against others, if we don't become aware of when we are doing it and shift it, we will end up trying to build a life that looks good instead of one that feels right. We will live our life from the outside-in, not from the inside-out.

We will lose ourselves in the fruitless pursuit of striving to be *above* humanity instead of among humanity, grasping for a sense of validation by 'outdoing' those around us. And we will pursue a path that we don't necessarily love, basing our worth and value off merits and credit and external appearances rather than the true value of our heart, our mind, and our soul.

When you lessen the grip that 'comparison-itis' has on you, you will discover YOUR true path and place here. You will focus on who *you* feel you are and who you were born to be. You will become driven by what you feel you are here to do and what you know in your heart you can do. You will do what you love and define what an authentic life looks like for you. You will quit comparing by realising that you are neither ahead nor behind those around you. In fact, you are not even in 'that' race.

Each person is unique and our greatest gift to ourselves is to find what lights *us* up and measure our fulfilment and successes on that instead: on how we feel day-to-day about who we are being and the life we are living. At the end of your life, that is what will matter to you. Questions of whether you earned more than Johnny or were more beautiful than Jill won't plague you. Your focus will be on what you made of *your* life; on whether you did what you dreamed of, for yourself and your loved ones.

So, if you feel that someone is better than you in some way, learn from them instead of feeling inferior beside them. Be inspired by their results. Use their growth and trajectory to fuel your own. Learn how they did what they did. Discover the secrets, the keys, the wisdom that helped them thrive. Allow their greatness to ignite yours, rather than constantly invalidating or minimising or writing yourself off whenever you see your gurus or heroes succeeding.

If you feel you are better than someone else, get back to work. Stop that! Remember that no matter how far you have come and how much you have done, there is always another mountain ahead of you, waiting to be climbed. This tends to be true when we are living deeply and consciously on purpose; that we will keep seeing new destinations to travel to and this doesn't stop until we draw our final breath.

If you focus on that next goal to conquer or next project to complete, you won't be cocky: you will be focused. You will be perfectly suspended between all that you have achieved so far, what you are working on, and where you are heading – and that is the journey of your life. Don't miss it by peeking over the fence at other people's lives, work, success, results, money.

The simple wisdom here is to invest your energy into your own life. Your own learning. Your own wisdom, skills, talents, and mastery. "Make your own bed," as Jordan B Peterson says. Be present in your own journey. Keep your head down with your heart and mind focused on your future, your next goal, your long-term legacy and vision. And love every single moment of this life – YOUR life – for what it is and every single part of yourself for who YOU are.

10
Hiding Your Gifts

"Your purpose in life is to use your gifts and talents to help other people. Your journey in life teaches you how to do that."

Tom Krause

The expression of your gifts is innately connected with the expression of your potential. They go hand-in-hand, like the stars and the night sky, heaven and Earth. Here's how it works. You are made of pure potential – the source of all that is and ever has been. That is where you came from, and it is what you are made of. You came into this world with something that you love to do and live to do, a calling which brings meaning to your life here. Your gifts are connected to that purpose.

The core of your potential, the pursuit of your purpose, and the expression of your gifts is the key that unlocks an extraordinary future for you. If you never acknowledge your potential, you will do and achieve less than what you are capable of. If you disconnect from your purpose, you will feel empty and depressed. And if you hold back your gifts, you will never know the life that is truly possible for you. I believe that you need all three to thrive in this world.

You can't build a career around your gifts, launch a successful business sharing them, earn an income from them, or become known for them if you don't use them, refine them, or put yourself and what you can do out into the spotlight: your writing, your art, your program, your speaking, your dancing, your business skills, your healing powers. The expression of your love and mastery is vital for your growth, goals, and dreams.

Here's an example. My gifts are writing and self-help. Packaging my skills and wisdom in both areas is what thoroughly, completely, and irreversibly changed my life and unlocked the future I dreamed of. My love of words and human potential has been the centrepiece, the essence, the foundation, and the heart of my entire career to date.

For nearly two decades, I have been living proof that sharing our gifts, putting them right out into the spotlight, is transformational. Empowering. Healing. Profound. I barely have words to describe the significance of expressing what we love and feel called to do, and I don't know where I would be if I had suppressed my gifts and held back from that innate knowing of a different life – the one I felt was awaiting me.

You *want* to do more with what is within you. So, why are you letting yourself be a best-kept secret? Are you taking for granted what you know, what you can do, or what you are good at? Do you assume that people aren't interested or won't want what you can offer? Are you so perpetually focused on mastery that you never stop and realise that what you can do today is already MORE than enough to change the world? Are you too humble to acknowledge your gifts or too shy to use them?

Perhaps you are too critical of yourself or too harsh on what you have done to *share* your work with people. Or perhaps you don't believe that you can be paid well for it and so you never try to earn a living from what you love to do. Or perhaps you are too busy doubting yourself and it interferes with you mastering your gift. Or perhaps you *are* incessantly comparing yourself to the talents of others and tripping yourself over in the process. Whatever the reason, be done with it – for good.

Your gifts exist for two reasons. First, they exist to enhance *your* life through immersing yourself in them, and secondly, they exist to enhance others' lives by you sharing them. It is a great, great blessing that what you love and live to do is both a source of healing for you and a source of value for humanity. It is often the key to our greatness.

People who express their gifts light up the world around them. When we see dancers, musicians, speakers, artists, chefs, athletes, and entrepreneurs showing up and doing their thing, it ignites us. We feel moved by their potential – and it is a reminder that we, too, have magic within us that is waiting to be practised, performed, and magnified. It is how we touch others by doing what we dream of.

It is miraculous what occurs in our lives when we apply ourselves; when we decide to transcend our human suffering, push past our problems, and do something original, profound, beautiful, and revolutionary from the soul. When we decide to make the most of our talents. When we choose to focus on our abilities instead of our shortcomings. When we focus on hope and vision and opportunity and get to work.

Working on our gifts and showing the world what we can do triggers profound personal growth. As you focus on your talents – on doing, pursuing, investing in, and mastering what you feel called to do – you transform. Your mind becomes focused. The noise of the world around you quietens down. Your emotions calm down. Your body buzzes with energy. Your thoughts centre around what you can do to reach a new level, to complete that project, to perfect your performance, to refine your product, to elevate your presence.

It is astonishing the effect doing what we love has on our body, mind, and spirit, and we need it far more than we often realise. It is only through and in the expression of our gifts that we can live the life we dream of, where we get to be ourselves fully in the world. So enough of not appreciating the full significance and power of what you have within you right now. Enough of hiding what you love, downplaying your genius, denying your intelligence, doubting your creativity.

It's time to use what you were born with and what you are skilled at as a tool to change lives, to make your unique impact, and to create your ripple for humanity. Other people *don't* do it the way you do. The world *does* need it. There is only one of you, and you only have one life. What are you waiting for? Get out there and DO YOUR THING!

11
ALWAYS ADULTING

"To live is the rarest thing in the world.
Most people just exist."

OSCAR WILDE

Are you allowing your responsibilities to drown out your dreams? Is your zest for life suffocating underneath the weight of an endless to-do list? Check your state and energy right now: have you become overly serious, worried, and conservative? When was the last time you were spontaneous? Do you allow your creative energy to run rampant sometimes? Or are you too busy following your head to follow your heart?

Perhaps you have been ignoring your calling, thinking that it is not logical or sensible to pursue your dreams. Maybe you have been filling your life with a long, long list of things you think you must do at the exclusion of what inspires you. Or maybe you keep putting what you feel you ought to do for others before what you *want* to do for yourself.

Although our responsibilities often have a great deal to do with the need for financial survival, it also extends far beyond our need to pay the bills and keep the lights on. Job obligations. Raising a family. Being there for a friend or partner. Social commitments. Taking care of elderly parents. Showing up for our community.

Our responsibilities can feel all-consuming. It's no wonder so many people are stressed out and miserable: they are living their life focused solely on what they feel they *have* to do, while deprioritising their own dreams. They have allowed themselves to be the very last item on their list, denying their desires and fast-tracking their way to emptiness and sadness.

I fell into this with the writing of this very book. I had delayed starting it because I was trying to be 'mature and responsible' for the sake of my business. I pushed back the writing of it for months, even though the idea had been tapping me on the shoulder and asking to be written. I was adulting, trying to do 'the right thing'… but then I remembered the power of our dreams and how the purpose of my life is to *write!* So, I took a leap of faith, and I dove in.

The words flowed, and within a day of starting the manuscript, I began attracting miracles. New paid-in-full clients, word-of-mouth referrals, and ideas for my programs started manifesting effortlessly in my life. My mood lifted, my heart opened, and my creativity skyrocketed. My cup was full, and my entire life benefited from it. *That* is the power of doing what we love: we become magnetic and inspired. What we *love* to do gives us energy for what we need to do.

To me, the pursuit of one's purpose and heartfelt vision is not just a 'nice' thing to do: it is crucial. It matters for our mental health, for our wellbeing, for our mood, for our spiritual connection, for our financial wealth, for our career, for our achievement, for our self-worth, and for our satisfaction.

For many, living life on purpose can even be the difference between wanting to live and wanting to die – it certainly was for me. Our purpose gives us a reason to apply ourselves, to grow, and to thrive. As we fulfil our dreams, we become a *greater* expression of ourselves, and thus an example to those around us of a completely different and refreshing approach to life.

Pursuing our vision, our mission, our inspiration, our love: this is how we unlock our gifts, set lofty ambitions, and achieve them. If we sacrifice this, the dream inside our heart and the reason for which we feel we were born, we will sacrifice *so* much. Too much. We will give up on what is, would, or could be possible – and surrender what our life is truly for.

The solution is not to ditch all your responsibilities and run, or to try and escape being an adult completely, although I know some people attempt it! Rather, it is to change our approach to adulthood so that we find a balance between what we *need* to do and what we *want* to do. It is working *on* your life as well as *in* your life so that you take care of what is important – that urgent paperwork, those essential tasks, those commitments – at the same time as you close the gap between your current life and your dream life.

It is to find a balance between what others need from us and what we want from our life. To do everything we can with what we have so that we continue to move in the direction we want. To schedule 30 minutes, an hour, a day, or three days a week to work on building our vision. To schedule our time exceptionally well so that we take care of business *and* ourselves. And to remember that we have far more choice in what we do with our time and energy than we often realise.

You don't have to spend your life resisting responsibility either. You can find a deep sense of meaning *through* what you do. You can fall in love with what you *need* to do at each stage of your life. You can *enjoy* that tax paperwork, the financial admin, the caring for a loved one, the housework, the gardening, the chores – and in a strange but beautiful way, it can become part of the tapestry of your dream, rather than a reason why you can't or won't live an extraordinary life.

The truth is that we will never escape the need to 'adult', and we will not ever be without responsibility. It's part of life. But if we live for our entire lives only doing what we think we have to or need to, we will crush the spirit within us that yearns to *play*: to explore, to try new things, to break the rules, to experience freedom.

You are not a victim of your circumstances. So, it is time to stop believing that you can only have this *or* that in life and start believing that you can have this *and* that. It's time to stop believing that handling of your responsibilities must come at the expense of your dreams. Realise and believe that you *can* grow your business while you work a job, that you *can* be the CEO of your company and still raise a family, that you *can* be a parent and still pursue your own interests. Giving up on any of these heartfelt aspirations is a choice.

Look to those who have managed to flow with their responsibilities and their ambitions, who haven't sacrificed their calling for their task list, who welcome the challenge of mastering their dreams and their duty. Let's follow their example and open our arms wide to embrace it all as part of our magnificent life. Don't let what is on your plate today extinguish the flame inside your heart.

12
Financial Survival

"Money is a reflection of your creativity, your capacity to focus, and your ability to add value and receive."

Tony Robbins

One of the greatest fears that causes us to hold back from unlocking our full potential is the fear that we either can't or won't make money doing what we love. It is the good old 'got-to-keep-the-lights-on' train of thought and "How will I survive financially?" question that holds far too many people in jobs and roles they either dislike or simply weren't born for.

This fear is a fight between survival and the spiritual calling within us. It is a battle between our responsibilities and our inspiration. It is a pull between our immortal soul – our higher self that knows we are destined to carve out an original life – versus our human self who sees bank balances and bills to pay. It is the "I can't because I have a family to provide for," reality and the "Who will want what I have to offer anyway?" story.

We often interpret this tension between our higher self and our human self as being 'logical'. Or we judge ourselves for being a daydreamer for wanting to pursue something that we *love*… and yet we were born for it. Why would you have gifts if they weren't meant to be shared?

And why would you have a dream burning inside your heart if it wasn't meant to be set free and pursued?

I believe that the problem with fears around financial survival isn't that we feel often overwhelmed by the need to stay safe, play it safe, or take the safe road; it is that we are missing a few key elements that would turn our dream into an everyday reality. We are often so afraid that we won't earn enough while pursuing our purpose that we never get *clear* on what that might look like: the plan of what we will offer, to whom, and for how much. And so, we never learn or master the professional skills required to commercialise our talents so others can benefit from it, and we can get paid for it.

In other words, we lack a practical strategy. We haven't put our business hat on yet to make *sure* we find a way to share what is within us with the world out there: the people who would love, who already need, and who will become raving fans of our original work. We haven't figured out how to package our value in a way that enables us to touch, move, inspire, support, and change lives in exchange for a sufficient or even an extraordinary payday.

I didn't have business skills when I first started out either. I was 'just' a 19-year-old writer who was obsessed with self-development and felt that she could make a difference. I just knew that I wanted to write, a thought that still brings tears to my eyes. I knew that I wanted to do what I loved and use what was within me to serve people.

Over the years, I learned business skills. I learned to package my gifts. I found ways to offer what I loved doing to the world. I learned to promote myself. I learned to speak from a stage. I learned marketing.

I learned to sell. I built my confidence and served people, earning income and empowering myself until I was well on my way. After a few short years, I had turned what I love into a living.

While I practised my writing skills, which was my primary focus and flow, I mastered the techniques that were not only beneficial but necessary for me to design and direct my own professional path. It's now been more than 15 years since I was employed in a job and there is no doubt in my mind that figuring out *how* to get paid for what I love – combined with my stubborn and steadfast determination to do well – was what made the difference.

Today, I am certain that unleashing our inner entrepreneur and acquiring business skills is one of the most important gifts we can give ourselves. It awakens our creativity, our desire for service, and our power and potential to be paid for our value, not just for the hours that we work.

A quick tip: if you are in a position where you dislike your job immensely, where it feels like your current work drains the life force out of you, or you would love to start your own business, do this for yourself. Set a short-term deadline, maybe six months, and save as much money as you can into a separate bank account. Make short-term sacrifices if you have to so that you can grow a cash cushion.

As tempting as it may be, don't allow yourself to touch that money for holidays or bills or any other reason: its sole purpose is to support you to start your business and to keep you safe and sane as you go through the (necessary) initial growth period. Having cash set aside in advance will mean that you do not have to skydive out of your current job without a financial parachute. It will keep your survival brain in a relaxed state so you can get creative and transition to where you would love to be. The sheer presence of that money will keep you calm enough to do the work you need to do to change your life forever. It will pay off!

It takes dedication to turn what we love doing into a living: a deep-seated drive to break out of the norm, the rat race, the misery and drudgery that so many people experience in their work-life and to *make* it for yourself. This is why your commitment is crucial if you are going to grow a purposeful and profitable career that you love with your whole heart, mind, body, and soul.

Your commitment will pull, push, nudge, and call you forwards on your path, inspiring and driving you to learn whatever you need to learn, hire whoever you need to hire, and persist through whatever challenges you face until the career, the business, the professional life you dream of *is* a reality. You won't succeed without that commitment – and those who have it in spades are those who not only replace their 9-to-5 income but reach levels of prosperity and influence they barely predicted when they first took that leap of faith.

Don't let the failure to even *try* to merge what you feel born to do and what you are paid to do be the reason that you don't find, carve out, persist with, and build a deeply rewarding career or business (or even businesses) for yourself. Be willing to *learn*, *grow*, and *expand* yourself so that you can experience what is possible for you in your vocation.

13
Emotional Baggage

"Eventually you will come to understand that love heals everything, and love is all there is."

Gary Zukav

Whether it feels as though your life is like a drama movie, you are continually overwhelmed by how you feel, or you simply feel weighed down by adversity from the past, there is no doubt that leaving your emotions unresolved will run or even ruin your life. Emotions tend to distract us, cause us to react irrationally to the events of our life, undermine our potential and progress, and blind us from the clarity we need for progress and fulfilment.

When we hold onto, obsess over, or hoard our emotions for too long, it blocks the flow in our life. It causes stagnation, frustration, dynamics, situations, phases, and cycles that we feel like we can't break out of. This can leave us believing that life is hard or that we are not, in fact, destined for greatness. It can affect our entire perception of ourselves and our experience of the world around us.

Unresolved grief weighs us down with sadness, causing us to lose ambition and feel stuck. Resentment and anger trigger bitterness, burning relationships, and causing our mind and body to become hot and toxic. Regret leaves us living in the past, causing us to miss the power and possibility of the present moment.

Shame causes us to hide from the world, retreating into a cocoon instead of living boldly in pursuit of what we LOVE. Pride closes our mind and limits our growth, causing us to do and achieve less than we are capable of. Hence, to go through life without processing your emotions about the events *of* your life can weaken your spirit and hold you back.

When we have a whole range of extreme emotions mixed together, we become highly charged. The smallest thing can set us off. We feel volatile and vulnerable inside our own life. We become easily triggered by events and news in the world around us. Our unresolved feelings about the past undermine our power in the now. All of the above makes it far more difficult to know who we are, to believe in who we are, to think clearly, to find solutions, to make rational decisions, to perform optimally, and to have foresight about our future.

You might think to yourself, 'It doesn't matter, though, does it? It's all in the past now.' But if it's not cleared, if you can't express genuine gratitude for the experience, if you wouldn't want to go through it again, if you still wish it had happened some other way, if you flinch at the thought of it, then it is not healed. We must realise that it *is* in the present if it is not cleared in the past.

If we don't know how to deal with a challenging event at the time it occurs, be it abuse, existential meltdowns, or other adversity, we tend to bury it. Why? Put simply, we do this out of survival. It is our animal instinct to escape and minimise the pain… and then we numb ourselves to the emotions we don't want to feel.

We try everything from compulsive shopping to overeating to excessive lovemaking to avoid being overcome by what we have tried for so long not to face and feel. I buried myself in huge amounts of work as a coping mechanism after my father passed away in 2022. His death was deeply confronting for me and despite knowing that his passing was approaching as he had been unwell for many years, it was one of the toughest experiences of my life. Needless to say, overworking wasn't the most effective pathway to process the regrets and grief I felt, and losing myself in my client work only prolonged my healing journey.

We can't leave our buried pain unaddressed – and deep down, you know that. You know that you can't continue allowing your future to be overshadowed, limited, or solely defined by your feelings about the past. Otherwise, your goals and dreams could be cut off at the knees, simply because you feel too hurt, too weak, too timid, too sore, or too worn out to try and create the future you love.

We tend to form personas, patterns, and behaviours surrounding our emotional wounding. Our pain – guilt, shame, resentment, regret, you name it – alters the way we act and what we do or don't do. This then becomes the new normal. It becomes "the way it is" or "the way we are" or even "who we are". When we resolve the emotions that affected us to begin with, those personas dissolve, the patterns change, and the behaviours shift. This sets us free to lead a different life – in some cases, dramatically so.

We see ourselves and treat ourselves differently. We see the world differently. We see the people in our life differently. We see the past, present, and future through new eyes. The love we feel is deeper. The drive to thrive is stronger. We do things differently because we feel differently, and this is how we change our life from the inside-out.

Emotions interfere with the course of our destiny when we either repress them completely or we become too immersed in how we feel and not focused enough on what we can do with our life. Neither extreme produces an inspiring outcome, as you either become stoic for years on end, bottling it all up inside, before finally cracking apart and experiencing a full-blown mental-emotional breakdown – or you become an emotional mess, triggered by every tiny disturbance or difficulty.

Wisdom is finding the middle line: a manageable pace of processing the emotions surrounding the significant events of your life. To achieve this, I recommend scheduling personal growth work into your calendar regularly; allocated, devoted time designed to help you peel back the layers, be that weekly, fortnightly, or at the very least, monthly. You can work through your feelings on your own by applying mindset tools or you can take the journey with a coach or mentor. As long as these sessions leave you feeling clearer, stronger, and grateful within yourself, that's all that matters.

So often, we are afraid of facing the shadows in our life; our history, our upbringing, all that which we have been through. But what we must come to terms with eventually is that the shadows also shape us, and a healthy fascination to heal your baggage will help to shed new light on the experiences of your life. This journey will gradually clear any wounding from your teenage years and childhood out of your adult energy field so you can act powerfully within your life and create what you would love.

It is true that you could probably spend a lifetime adventuring through the deepest corners of your psyche and outer reaches of your 'self'. I also know that you don't want your entire life to be consumed by extensive psychoanalysis and therapy. You want to LIVE. You want to do things, conquer things, create things, build things, express things, try things, experience things. So, do both: prioritise your healing work and your action steps. Work towards your dreams and break through what holds you back as you go. Act and heal at the same time. That is where the real you will be unleashed.

Remember: those boxes don't get unpacked if we don't unpack them. So, shed the baggage that weighs you down. Transcend the trauma. Address how you *feel* so you can *be, do, and become* what you dream. Find the light in the darkness. And finally, recognise when a wound or story has run its course so that you can set yourself free from the past, lead your own life, and move powerfully into the future.

14
Rescuing Humanity

"When we rescue people from the consequences of their actions, we rob them of facing reality. Reality is life's wisest teacher."

Anonymous

I understand what it is like to feel struggle in the world around you. I know that heartache of hearing stories of adversity, where people have encountered a challenging turn of events or an unexpected illness or the sudden death of a loved one. And I am well familiar with the wave of empathy that one might feel when simply realising how many human beings feel lost, burned out, and worthless.

It can sting to bear witness to the condition of people's lives, bodies, countries, and bank accounts, to see people being killed, giving up on their dreams, going through break-ups, break-ins, abuse, or bankruptcy. It takes just five minutes of reading news headlines to learn about the problems that humanity is facing or a moment of conversation with a friend, customer, or family member to discover the difficulty they are facing or the questions they are grappling with. You may experience a desire to save others from the pain they are experiencing.

It is a mirror of your heart that you want to see perfect strangers and the ones you love thriving instead of being weighed down and broken by overwhelming challenges. It is a reflection of your character that you *care* about humanity deeply. And it says a great deal about your spirit and your love, that you want people to break through, to have *more*, to beat down their obstacles, and live a freer life.

It is far from easy to witness people burned out by work, defeated by a divorce, or fighting to get through the next day. But the wisdom here is that we benefit by being conscious of *who* we help and *how* we help them. If we aren't, then as we jump into the water to save them, we can drown in the process.

Maintaining this healthy balance between ourselves and others in this way ensures that we don't become so weighed down by the heaviness of it all that we can barely move. The goal is to *serve* people, not save them. It is to help others live the life they dream about at the same time as you create and experience the life *you* dream about.

The following are signs that you may be attempting to rescue humanity. You discount your services to the point where you either can't survive or you are working for free, putting yourself into financial struggle. You give your money to others freely – charities, friends, family – but leave yourself in a hole of debt. You spend significant amounts of time and energy giving advice to or helping friends, at the cost of making progress on your own meaningful goals. You help others get ahead but leave yourself behind.

Other signs could be staying in a relationship longer than you want to because you are afraid of whether your partner will survive without you. Attempting to 'fix' your partner. Sidelining your priorities. Holding back on what you want for someone else. Feeling sorry for every person you see who is battling. Being afraid to say 'No'. Pushing your needs aside the moment someone needs something from you. Being overly emotionally invested in the outcomes of those around you. The list goes on – and only you will know how and how much *you* have been trying to save people.

There *is* undeniably a time for contribution in life – and I also know that it can be one of the most meaningful things you do. My close-knit network and I raised $7,000 in three days at the start of 2021 to help my girlfriend Laraib Malik in Pakistan pay for her first-year medical school fees, and it brought me to tears with every dollar we raised. The trick is to keep your philanthropic efforts in a healthy balance where you take care of you *and* others, instead of falling into the pattern of caring for you *or* others. The vision is wellbeing for all, not just the few.

Dissolving your desire to rescue humanity doesn't mean that you will charge outrageous amounts of money for every little thing that you do for your clients or never be available for loved ones when they need support. It just means that you take care of yourself in equal measures. It means that you become *conscious* of your 'giving' efforts and make sure that they flow from the heart, not from a yearning to rescue the weak or be seen as a saviour.

One of my mentors, Dr John Demartini, teaches that we only try to save in others what we have wounding on in ourselves. In essence, what we have unresolved pain over in our life, we try to rescue other people from in *their* life. For example, if you felt invisible or insignificant as a child, you will tend to try and make other people feel seen, heard, and valued. Or if you struggled with your academics as a teenager, you either dumb yourself down to make others feel smarter or you go out of your way to educate others.

Reflect on this now. How often do you try to rescue others? Where does your desire to rescue people come from? Who do you typically try to rescue and why? What drives that in you? Does it give you the feeling that you are needed? Are you seeking a sense of belonging? Approval? Meaning? What is incomplete in your own life that you are trying to fix vicariously through helping others? What pain are you attempting to remove in the world around you?

There is a difference between living a life of service – where you are devoted to making your difference and leaving a legacy – and living your life so caught up in carrying, taking on, and worrying about the problems in others' lives that you sacrifice your wellbeing and resources at the drop of a hat to save someone.

Yes, allow others to share in the blessings of your life, and even a portion of your wealth. Send prayers to those who are hurting. But be sure to put the oxygen mask on yourself first. Don't forget that each person is on a journey of evolution and growth and, even if you can't see it right now, they *are* being guided and blessed on their path.

You are an equally valuable part of humanity too, an equally worthy child of this universe, and you also deserve to flourish. You too deserve to be picked up when you fall or encouraged to move forwards on your path. You too deserve riches, progress, accomplishment, wellness, freedom, lightness, beauty, awe, and love. Truly. You are no good to the world if you are so burned out from saving others that you forgot to save yourself.

So, choose your contribution to this world consciously and remember that fulfilling your dreams in the greatest way possible *is* an act of love for humanity because, from that empowered place, you can reach out or back or down and give a hand up to those people who need it.

15
BURNOUT

"Give up the delusion that burnout is the inevitable cost of success."

ARIANNA HUFFINGTON

Do you feel like everything is piled on top of you right now? Are you weighed down by a long list of problems you haven't managed to solve? Does it all feel like it is just too much? As you read this, you might be feeling so burned out and under such immense amounts of pressure that your spark for life feels like it has been all but snuffed out.

You have been doing, doing, doing. Pushing yourself to exhaustion. Burning the candle at both ends. You feel as though you can't rest and that you have to do even *more* to survive or succeed. Perhaps you have high achiever syndrome, where you feel compelled to do bigger and better every day… and you are wiped out. Amidst this struggle, unleashing your potential seems like the last thing you can do. Your cup is so profoundly empty, it has barely got a drop left in it.

I understand. I have been there. I know that profoundly deep spiritual tiredness, mental fatigue, and physical exhaustion from trying to do and manage it all. I also know there is a road back to your vital, creative, funny, and lively self who *loves* life. So, if you feel that you are breaking apart right now, breathe deeply for a moment… and then let's unpack your burnout so that you can begin to heal.

Burnout is typically caused by trying to do too much or by trying to solve too many things at once. Trying to do too much is self-evident: you are trying to take it all on without acknowledging what you can realistically achieve within the limits of your body, your mind, and time. You have said "Yes" to far too many things (or to too many big things) at the same time, and now you are suffering.

Whether you did this out of stubbornness, a desire to prove your strength, or simply because you were overly enthusiastic about your capabilities, it is time to let something go. It is time to channel your energy into the few projects that matter greatly – the ones that can move the needle in your life and career. To lighten the load, feel your flow return, and watch your results start to manifest.

Trying to solve too many things at once means you are expecting yourself to figure out the answer to two, three, five, or ten issues simultaneously… and you are failing. It is a fast path to mental burnout and decision fatigue. Instead of thinking you have to build Rome in a day, try this. Write your problems down. Pick the most pressing issue. Then work on it until it is resolved. Take your time. Even enjoy the process. I promise that you will move forward faster and, as a bonus, you will likely find that solving the first problem helps you to solve the others as well.

Let's also examine the idea that achieving your dreams has to be an endless struggle or that we have to break ourselves apart in order to break through. Where did you pick that up? Was it from the movies? From stories of hardship? From a mentor? From your parents? And is it what you truly believe and feel deep down? That you must work hard constantly to progress and that there *is* no easier way to thrive?

Over the years, I have heard several leaders say that anything worth working for is difficult – and I don't disagree. But my personal belief is that achieving one's dreams is a perfect balance of hustle and heart. In other words, you put your nose to the grindstone while also feeling worthy of the endless stream of support that life provides us as we seek to fulfil our destiny. It is human and heaven together that make great things happen.

To fly, we must believe that we were born for big things, that we are capable of big things, and that, yes, we are blessed and highly favoured, as my friend Georg Galas often says. It is not egotistical but rather healthy to let go of what is not our calling and to allow life to do some of the heavy lifting to build the dream. Otherwise, we will spend our lives in a perpetual state of burnout, pushing ourselves to mental, physical, or personal breakdown.

After opening my company, I began working seven days a week. It only took a year before cracks started to show and I burned out. Despite generating six-figure revenues every year, I realised that I needed a different approach and that both my brain and my body required support.

I realised that I couldn't sustain that work speed or intensity for the rest of my life and nor did I want to. I had to slow down – and the effort to halve my work pace was worth it. Now I am wiser: I listen to my body daily which allows me to recognise the warning signs, adjust my output, and avoid burnout long before it happens.

Deep down you know this, but I am here to remind you that you are HUMAN – not superhuman. Your body is not a machine. You can't flog your system endlessly without paying a price. As much as you might wish it to be otherwise, you can only solve, master, and overcome one thing at a time. You are here to find what you love *most*, to make your impact by being *you*, not by trying to be it all to the world around you.

When you are in the thick of burnout, feeling overwhelmed and worn thin, it can seem difficult to dream about your future. You may have reached a point where fulfilling your purpose seems impossible or unrealistic. Or you just feel too damn tired to get to work on what is in your heart. But please know that this feeling is just temporary. As you recover from your burnout – one day at a time – your drive *will* return.

So, be gentle with yourself. Start to make your way from burnout to balance. Eliminate that which no longer serves or inspires you. Nurture your body deeply, every day. Manage your energy. Slow it all down. Make time for healing. Simplify your life, your work, your business model, your routine so that you can find peace in your mind and start to make progress on what matters.

Give yourself the time and space you need to find your heart again, to remember why you started on this path and what you set out to achieve. You CAN overcome this. You WILL overcome this. The light will shine again. You will feel lighter again – sooner than you think.

16
OVERWHELM

"Success is sequential, not simultaneous."

GARY KELLER

Overwhelm is not only the cousin, but often the source of burnout. It is the cause of the effect. Overwhelm is the experience of feeling that it is just all too much to handle and that there isn't enough of you to go around. You are pushing yourself to the limit and redlining just to get through the days. You are buried underneath a huge pile of work and responsibilities and there seems to be no light at the end of the tunnel.

Your stress levels have skyrocketed. You have little to no time and space for yourself to defrag let alone recover. Your nervous system is wound up, leaving you feeling constantly on edge, worn out, emotional, and jittery. When taken to an extreme, this can cause anxiety, breakdown, and depression, not to mention illness in the body. How can you fulfil your dream when you are breaking apart under the weight of it all?

Similar to burnout, committing our energy and time to too many things is typically the cause of overwhelm. Out of enthusiasm or obligation, we say "Yes" to this, that, and the other. Then, after we have said "Yes" one too many times, we then expect ourselves to handle it all simultaneously – and not only that but do *well* at all of it. Easy, right?

Dissolving overwhelm and avoiding the burnout that often follows starts by first acknowledging that feeling overwhelmed is seldom an invitation to push even harder. In fact, overwhelm is feedback to let you know that yes, you *are* redlining. It is the warning light on the dashboard to let you know you are headed for a crash if you don't slow down and take your car in for a service.

It is a Post-it note from your mind and body to let you know that this approach you have to your life and work isn't sustainable. Is the way you are living and working bringing out the best in you? Are you fulfilling your potential? Or are you running around like a chicken with its head cut off trying to get by and get ahead? While being in a perpetual state of overwhelm can give off the impression that you are giving it all you've got, it is likely counterproductive to what you are trying to achieve.

It's important to recognise that we are often the main cause of our own overwhelm. It is highly likely that you have been doing this to yourself; that you have been stressing yourself out and tying yourself in knots unnecessarily. The good news? This means you are also the one with the power to change it – and here's the approach I suggest for getting started.

Take ten minutes to list out everything that is on your plate or on your mind right now. Write it all out: the commitments, the projects, the concerns, the loose ends, and the open loops in your personal and professional life. Then, take a step back. Walk away for an hour, a day, or a week. Take a breather to collect yourself and let the dust settle. This is also a prime opportunity for self-care, to carve out time to do something that nourishes, warms, and reenergises you. Day spas, a week off, a deep sleep, dinner with friends, and listening to music are equally beneficial ways to fill your cup again.

Then, come back to your list and revisit it with one objective: to find the top priority. What will produce the most progress or bring you the greatest fulfilment? If you dedicated all of your energy, time, and focus to it, what would move your life forwards most? Identify the main objective, the most important project, the critical focus.

Now, review the remaining items on your list to highlight what you can let go of. What commitments can you withdraw from? Which obligations could you release for now? What invitations can you politely decline? Revisit your calendar, your business plan, and your social life, and find a way to make space for yourself. Ask yourself if each thing that has your attention right now, also has the power to change your life. Harness your self-love to complete this process. Create the breathing room that you *need*, before you breakdown completely.

As you work through this process, you *will* reach a point where you experience a sigh of relief. You will literally feel the pressure reduce and your mind and body will relax. The stress will start dissolving. You will shift from feeling like "I can't do this" to "I *can* handle that." You have let go to create flow so you can function again. Where before your commitments felt unmanageable or impossible, you now know what to do and how to conquer what lies before you.

Now you can schedule your life with your top priorities as the centrepiece, blocking out time in your calendar to do, master, and complete *one* vital thing at a time. Although it has sometimes been preached as a powerful skill to have, multitasking only causes further unwanted stress as it fragments your attention, dilutes your focus, overloads your energy, and delays your progress. Clarity, simplicity, and focus are your keys to success.

It takes courage to admit that we can't do it all or that we need reprieve so we can breathe again – but it is necessary. No great leader or business owner or Olympic athlete did it all themselves nor did they achieve greatness overnight. In fact, it is often *because* they narrowed their focus and picked a worthy singular goal at the expense of all else that they succeeded at all.

I get it: you are ignited and inspired by your goals, and you want to achieve it all right this second. But you don't want the pursuit of your purpose or the fulfilment of your dreams to be a defeating source of overwhelm either; you can't fulfil your potential that way. Optimise the bandwidth you have by working on one pivotal change or milestone in each stage, knowing that it all adds up to the life and legacy inside your heart. As Gary Keller said, "Success is sequential, not simultaneous."

We achieve anything worthy, significant, or great in small steps: paragraphs become a book, PT sessions become a body transformation, practices become a performance, sales become a million-dollar business. Your dreams are the result of many, many small actions together, and if it all feels too much or too big, you can't manage it – which means you can't master it.

Day by day, we build our destiny and as much as you want to do everything right now and get there faster, your life is a journey you don't want to miss out on. So, stay true to what you need to do first. Honour yourself and your priorities. And master the art of doing exactly the right amount at exactly the right time so you can build the career you dream of one step at a time.

17
High-Achiever Syndrome

"Be not afraid of greatness. Some are born great, some achieve greatness, and some have greatness thrust upon them."
William Shakespeare

To all those restless souls who feel born to *do* great things, who keep pushing forward no matter what, who struggle to take days off... hello! I wrote this for you. I know the endless obsession with one's work and the desire to reach for new levels intimately. I also know that regardless of where our pig-headed determination to excel stems from, if we don't learn to manage it, it may very well be the cause of our demise, a source of unfulfillment, and detrimental to the very dream we originally set out to achieve.

The deep-seated mental, emotional, and psychological pressure to succeed has both a curse and a blessing within it. The curse is that you live a life of work, grind, and hustle. The relentless pursuit for greatness, for excellence, and for achievement can easily lead to burnout.

We can work seven days a week or years on end without feeling that it is 'enough'. We rarely feel that we are 'there', because to a high achiever, there is always more that we can do: there is another mountain to climb, another goal to hit, another race to run, another book to write (ha!).

We jump from one milestone to the next, pushing ourselves constantly, rarely resting, all the while measuring and comparing ourselves at every turn to our past results and the people around us. Ironically, our desperate search for success can cause us to struggle, flail, and fail instead of rising and thriving inside our purpose.

The blessing is that you will live a life dedicated to the continual discovery of your potential: of what you can do, of what you are capable of. The drive to do more ignites you and pushes you to reach entirely new levels and standards, to travel to new horizons and fulfil new visions.

Obsessed with the notion of achievement, you will be stubbornly persistent to do your best work, applying yourself in a life that is anything but lazy and likely growing an extraordinary career in the process. If you *do* manage to stop occasionally along the way, smell the roses, and appreciate yourself for all that you have done – for your superhuman effort – the depth of the love and respect you will feel for yourself will be unparalleled and humbling, to say the least.

The question then becomes, how do we strike a healthy approach to high achievement? Where we back ourselves towards extraordinary results while simultaneously loving ourselves no matter what the outcome may be? So that we perform and rise without crushing ourselves under the weight of the overwhelming expectation to go big or go home?

We seek to master these two profound truths. First, that you are totally, wholly and completely worthy of love, no matter what you do or do not achieve. Just by breathing, you are valuable, and your worth as a human being cannot be measured solely on the level of fame you rise to, the fortunes you accumulate, or the records you break. Do you believe it? Or, like me, do you feel that the value of who you are rests partly (or largely) on how impressive your accolades, your impact, your bank balance?

The irony of high achievement is that we can so easily tie the meaning of our life to what we do or have done. Yet to propel ourselves to even greater heights, we must reconnect with that unconditional love within us, the inner self who doesn't rank us on how many A's we got, but who just *loves* and wants the absolute best for us. That love, the one unhindered by ideas of who you should be or what you could do, is the one that fills your cup and calls you to the next level of your own life. Without that love, you will not only burn out but rely on your accolades to boost your sense of worth.

The second wisdom to embrace is that we often thrive the *most* when we are doing what we do because we *love* it. We don't build a business or get a degree or make a million because it's 'cool'. We do it because it is rooted inside our soul, at the very core of who we are. Because we feel called to and moved to by the spirit within us, because it feels like an inherent and predestined part of our life on Earth. That is where truly meaningful achievement lives: within our heart.

Just because you *can* do it and just because someone else says you *should* do it doesn't mean you *have* to do it. Tricky, I know, especially if the world or the people around you value what you do: the thing you *can* do but don't feel born to do. But at the end of the day, who are you living for?

Begin to work not for the end goal but for the sheer privilege of doing it. THAT is the work the world needs from you the most – not *everything* but your *one thing* – and it is this work that will most likely transform your life and career in the process. The work that is infused with your soul, your personality, your essence.

Instead of trying to do it all and do it all well, all the time, realise that *less is more* when it comes to your goals and your dreams. As we explored in the previous chapter, this means channelling more of your precious energy into fewer pursuits. Relinquish that which you don't love, what does not or no longer lights you up. Identify the areas where you are unusually gifted and double down on them. Apply yourself to your soulful mission, without attempting to be best in class at everything you try your hand at.

Instead of burning yourself out and burying yourself under the pressure to succeed, ask yourself what the most important and meaningful achievement of your life would be, and then surrender to it. Channel your heart, your efforts, your genius, into the legacy, the meaningful pursuit, and the soulful purpose that lights you up and allow it to guide your journey.

And finally, open your heart towards yourself the way you would embrace a child and think about this: what would your younger self say if they met you today? Don't you think they would look up to you as a hero, amazed at all that you have done and in awe at who you have become?

I guarantee that the seven-year-old self (who still exists within you) wouldn't look at your results and think you were lagging behind. They would think you are badass, no exception. So, acknowledge your immense efforts, thank yourself for your fiery determination to make the most of your life, and let your appreciation for the past fuel your trajectory for the future.

18
Failure Focus

"Success is not final; failure is not fatal.
It is the courage to continue that counts."

Winston Churchill

Working hard for years and not reaching where you want to be. Feeling like you have given it your all and it simply wasn't enough. Dedicating enormous amounts of effort, time, and energy into a project or business or career path that hasn't paid off yet. Trying for so long and never quite achieving what you yearn for. It is disheartening.

The road to the top can try and test us at the best of times and, after what feels like endless attempts to break through to the next level, we can end up sitting in the corner, feeling defeated by the pursuit of our own aspirations. This focus on failure can lead to a drastic change in our attitude towards life, as we slowly lose our enthusiasm and even become cynical about our purpose, dreams, and goals.

But you and I both know that beating yourself up or wondering if you should just give up doesn't help. It drains your energy and interferes with you bouncing back, becoming stronger, and finally achieving what is inside your heart. We cannot move forwards if we are fixated on the past, nor can we take bold and hopeful strides towards what we want if we are constantly kicking ourselves while we are down. We must back ourselves in every way that matters if we are to live a life that counts.

If you have been focused on your failures to the point where it's self-defeating, then it's worth considering that you are being impatient with your journey. Simply put, you think that you should have achieved (*insert goal here*) by now, but the truth is that it takes longer than you thought to become an overnight success. Your unrealistic expectations cause you to feel deflated by the process that is *necessary* for you to hit it big.

This impatience – the sense of urgency to do it all NOW or feeling that you are behind on your own dreams – can cause you to avoid the real work that is required to see your vision through to fruition. It can result in skipping important steps and rushing vital tasks, which will only delay your progress.

Do you have a sense of entitlement about your success, thinking or feeling that you should have it immediately without putting in the hard yards first? Brutal to ask, I know. But it is important to reflect on this for yourself, just in case you are unknowingly expecting life to move mountains for you without you picking up a shovel.

The other possibility to consider is the reason that you *haven't* succeeded yet is that you haven't done the one thing that you know will change it all yet. You already know what I'm referring to. The strategy you haven't tried yet. The skill you haven't learned yet. The action you haven't taken yet. The idea you have had for months but haven't done anything with yet. You *do* know what to do next to elevate your life and career and wealth to the next level… maybe you just haven't done it yet. In which case, when will be the right time to do it?

Sometimes we feel like a failure because we are measuring our results against someone else's progress, status, or achievements. Are you comparing yourself to someone who is running a completely different race from you? Who or what are you measuring yourself and your precious life against? And, more importantly, would you *really* swap your life for theirs? You are unique as is your journey, and because of this, it is impossible to say that you are more or less successful than anyone else. Instead, focus on what *you* can do to transform *your* life, what you can do to make your dreams come true.

Remembering why you began your journey is a powerful antidote to the feeling of failure. Perhaps it is time to remember why you first started out on your current path. Reflecting on your original vision will refresh your enthusiasm and reignite your love for what you do. There is infinite inspiration – for effort, for discipline, for resilience, for accomplishment – within your own heartfelt dream. In fact, reconnecting with what you initially set out to do may be all the inspiration you need to get back on your feet with renewed vigour and courage.

Perhaps it is time to debrief what you think you failed at, take the lessons from what didn't work, and *move on*. Focus on these coming years being bigger and brighter than whatever happened yesterday. Become more invested in what *can* be rather than what *was*. Shift your attention towards your future. Turn your head towards tomorrow. Allow whatever you do next to be called by your heart and soul, not driven by pain from the past.

You don't need to 'make it' to prove to yourself that you aren't a loser, nor do you need to achieve greater things to make up for what didn't work out yesterday. Just start where you are and BUILD. Transform. Create. Get to work. Reflect. Heal. Educate yourself. Apply yourself. Rise. Appreciate your journey – the one you live every day – instead of drowning it out with expectations about where you thought you'd be by now.

Your journey will be long, and this is why it matters greatly that you acknowledge your progress in each phase. Be specific about your goals so that you can not only recognise when you achieve them but also appreciate your momentum and growth in all of its subtle forms. Celebrate the milestones on the path to reach the goal, not just the goal itself.

If you feel frustrated that your life is changing too slowly, look at the bigger picture. Remember why you are here on Earth. Put this stage of your journey into a higher perspective. Reignite the dream inside your heart. Do what you love often. No matter how rough the road, find it inside yourself to pick yourself up and keep moving. Strike a balance between being gentle on yourself and pushing yourself to new levels.

You could give up and walk away… but is that what you want? Yes, you might feel defeated in this moment, but you are never defeated while you still have the vision in your mind, the dream in your heart, and life on your side. Stay focused on your path: on what you need to do to get to where you want to go. If you do this, if you remain devoted and diligent and determined, it is impossible not to make progress down the path you feel called to follow.

We must put ideas of failure out of our mind in order to see our success to fruition. The fulfilment of our dreams must be our only option… and then we must trust in life without resistance to guide us there. We must view each moment as a stepping stone rather than a stumbling block, so that we become exactly the kind of person who achieves exactly what we dream of. That is the way to flourish.

19
LOW SELF-WORTH

"One of the greatest tragedies in life is that you will always be loved more than you will ever know."

ALAN WATTS

Of all the internal obstacles we can dismantle, the invisible limitations we can defeat, and the personal growth work we can do to create the life we dream of, strengthening and deepening our self-worth may be the most important. Why? Because your relationship with yourself determines what you will experience in the future.

In fact, your self-worth is reflected in each moment of your life. Your outer world is a mirror of how you feel about yourself on the inside. If you are beating yourself up, judging yourself, or punishing yourself, these inner battles will appear in your daily reality as self-sabotage; little or big ways in which you undermine your wellness or delay what you dream of.

If you are upset with yourself – because there is a part of you or something you did in the past that you haven't made peace with – then you will likely experience great struggle on your path. You will battle with setting boundaries, bend yourself to please others, and put yourself last. You won't do what you love or prioritise your holistic fulfilment in life. I daresay, even your physical health will suffer from an absence of unconditional self-love.

Your war with yourself will appear manifest as a job that drains you, relationships where you don't feel appreciated, and financial hardship. Why does this happen? Because you haven't *allowed* yourself to have fulfilling work, deeply meaningful relationships where you are adored and respected, and a flow of abundance. It is sometimes the most difficult truth but it is the simple truth: we must love ourselves if we are to thrive.

Regardless of how strong your self-worth is, you *will* face challenges. That is inevitable. But the difference is that when your relationship with yourself is robust, you will overcome problems faster. Instead of accepting a painful outcome because deep down, you don't feel that you deserve better and that it was your fate to suffer all along, you will focus on what is beyond the obstacle and find a way forwards. You will refuse to be crushed in the face of trials and tribulations, heartache and heartbreak, and you will express great self-devotion.

Self-devotion is self-love in motion. Self-love is a state of being, and self-devotion is the expression of that. It is devotion to finding your purpose and fulfilling it, and devotion to turning your life around and doing it. Whatever those big changes are that you know you need to make, your self-love will give you the courage and the strength to do them; to reinvent yourself, to transform your career, to overhaul your business, to leave that relationship (or start a new one), to heal your body, to move cities, to launch yourself into a whole new life.

Your self-love IS the key: a love for yourself that is so deep that you have no fear in opening your heart for how far you have come and how hard you have fought to be who and where you are. That love is the healing you need. It is the encouragement you require. It is the fuel to your Ferrari. It is the reason to fight for your dreams, to speak your truth, to create a life that both *works* for and brings out the best in you.

By the way, there is no doubt in my mind that unhindered self-love is also the seat of financial empowerment. In fact, I believe that deep inside we all have the desire to flourish financially and that the greater our love for ourselves, the more likely we are to create wealth. In your heart, you *want* to take care of yourself, provide for yourself, and give yourself what you dream of – whether that is a travelling lifestyle or building a fortune to pass on to future generations.

When your self-worth is strong, you will not only feel deserving of the money that you have earned and will earn in the future, but you will also have the discipline required to do what it takes to set yourself up for life. Your healthy inward relationship with yourself will express itself outwardly in a healthy relationship with money.

You will fall in love with money in a new way, where organising your financial paperwork becomes a joy, where creating an investment plan feels like a gift, and where paying bills feels like a privilege. Instead of dodging the difficulty and living a financially impoverished life, you will master wealth for yourself. That is what strong self-worth will inspire you to do.

The fastest way to grow rock-solid self-worth is to be honest with yourself about what you don't love or appreciate about who you are – and love it. We are often so focused on presenting a highlight reel of ourselves – on social media, to our loved ones, to our partner, our friends, our customers, and followers – that we never end up confronting or loving what I humorously nickname the 'sewage reel'. What is the sewage reel? It is the list of things that you don't love yourself for. You know, the ones that you try and hide from the world around you.

You know those habits, those body features, those past experiences and behaviours that make you cringe when you think of them? Those things you still feel ashamed of or guilty for? Your perception of them is what causes the suffering in your life. Your judgements on yourself cause resistance between what you want and what you have. They interfere with your growth and are the reason why you sabotage your aspirations and never quite 'get there'.

Your lack of love towards yourself, for all parts of yourself, is what creates the invisible barrier between where you are and the life you yearn for. And so, if you are ready to improve your self-worth, start there. One by one, love each aspect of yourself, each stage and phase of your life, and seek to understand and love rather than judge yourself for what you have done or not done.

Spending your life beating yourself up is no way to live. How can what you want manifest with relative ease and grace if you don't fundamentally feel worthy of it? How can your wildest dreams bloom and blossom if your garden is full of weeds? It is time to bury the hatchet, to make peace with yourself on the deepest level. To open your heart and embrace your true self. This is how you unleash your potential and fulfil it.

Love IS the answer. Deep, unconditional, unrestricted love for yourself; for the human God made you to be; for the person you were designed to be. You are a gift to this world and it's time to realise it because that is how you will attract, experience, create, and build the life and career you dream of.

20
Control Complex

"The moment of surrender is not when life is over. It's when it begins."
Marianne Williamson

There is enormous power in this universe, a force far beyond us. It is the spirit and the source and the fire of creation. It is the very essence of life itself. I believe that this very power, this force, wants to express itself through you. It wants to flow through you and move you to do extraordinary things in this world, with your life. It wants you to fulfil a heartfelt and powerful destiny on Earth, but you cannot do this if you are trying to control everything. Like kinking a garden hose, trying to control every event and outcome restricts your flow and limits both your possibility and your potential.

The urge to control the people and situations we encounter typically stems from deep-seated fear. If you are gripped by fear in your mind and body – the fear of survival, the fear of being hurt, the fear of being weak – then you may try to control the events of your life in an attempt to avoid the pain you fear.

For example, unresolved pain from relationship break-ups or family wounding or a rough childhood or being beaten up earlier in your journey often causes a fear of being vulnerable. You may try to become tough to avoid being in a position of weakness again. You may try to control life by dodging uncomfortable situations or by handling circumstances or people with an unnecessarily aggressive approach.

The trauma that causes your fear and thus your instinct to control may also be a result of experiencing elevated levels of stress for an extended period of time. Perhaps you have had so much on your plate for years on end that you had to develop control strategies just to cope with it all. Examples of this might be pushing yourself past the point of burnout, rarely carving out downtime, refusing to delegate, and having walls so high that no help can get in. Underneath it all, there exists a terror that if you slow down or stop, both you and your life will fall apart.

We use these coping mechanisms over and over for such a long time that it becomes our default response to life's events. We constantly worry that we won't make it, try to maintain a tight grip on everything at the same time, and feel easily anxious if something doesn't quite go to plan. We are so tightly wound and stressed that there is no room for flexibility let alone transformation or miracles. Then, even if and when the pressure on us is eventually alleviated, we still rely on these same habitual coping mechanisms in our work and life. Regardless of the source, excessive attempts to control the world around us end up running our lives, likely making us wildly miserable in the process.

When you heal the underlying wound that causes the desire to control everything and everyone around you – whether that is childhood trauma or adulthood stress – you will experience what is *beyond* a life of control: a deep, deep TRUST in yourself that you have your back and a trust in life that *it* has your back.

Imagine the sweetness, the miracle, the blessing of being able to relax and live curiously, instead of being consumed by pain and fear. It is extraordinary to live in the mystery, in the discovery of what life is, in the exploration of who we are, of love and truth, in the beauty, depth, and power of the present moment. You will relax and your life will start to flourish – trust in that.

This might be an edgy topic, but I feel compelled to write about it as I am, after all, a modern-day woman. Traditionally, women were housewives and mothers. Today, however, women have far more possibility and opportunity available to us. We can also run businesses, lead empires, and become wealthy in our own right, expressing ourselves far more freely and fully as we chart the course of our own life.

But sometimes (and I write this with immense love, because I did it, too), and especially if we have experienced personal heartbreak or pain in our social lives, we can take it to the extreme, where we step so far into the traditionally masculine roles of money, career, and business, that we shut off our feminine flow entirely.

We can become hardened by our pain, and this can trigger us to go into 'over-control mode'. We then tend to repress the desire for support, partnership, and connection – all those lovely things that, in turn, add the colour to life. We think and 'do' while forgetting to relax and feel. We end up shrouding our feminine radiance in a cloak of masculine strength.

I am a huge advocate for female empowerment and there is no doubt that we are far more capable in traditionally masculine tasks and roles than was ever thought 100 or so years ago – and what a gift that is.

But what I have also discovered in my own personal journey is that letting *go* of control is just as vital to our wellbeing and our potential as stepping in, stepping up, getting organised, and leading our lives.

There is evidently a lesson for us all in this and it is a lesson in softening. In opening to the feminine essence within us. In taking the walls down. In receiving. In admitting vulnerabilities and expressing true feelings. In allowing. In sitting with our feelings comfortably. In showing up authentically in all aspects of our lives. In letting *go* of control a little (or a lot) so that we can let *life* in.

What would a more fulfilling relationship with life look like for you? Is it time to think less and feel more? To trust in yourself, that you will know what to do and when? That you can and will provide exactly what you need and want for yourself? To stop trying to be the general manager of the universe? To *let* it happen as much as you *make* it happen? What would it be like if you lived in the mystery, open-minded and open-hearted to life? Imagine that. Feel it. Breathe into it.

Gaining control and influence over the important things in your life is essential – your financial situation, your estate, your team, your business, your health – but if you try to micromanage every little thing, it will only cause rigidity and stress for you.

You cannot control the weather, people's opinions, people's actions, the future of technology, or what will happen in the world tomorrow. But what you can control is what you do, your emotional healing, your personal growth, your health and wealth habits, how you develop your character, your spiritual connection, and your philosophy towards life… and it is in *this* where you will find your mastery.

21
Time Management

"It is not enough to be busy. The question is: what are we busy about?"
Henry David Thoreau

Every single person who walks the Earth lives within the human construct of time. For many, time is a source of stress generally caused by not having enough of it, running out of it, or not doing what we want to with the time we have been given. We push against it, feel constricted by it, worry that we are wasting it, or wish we could do more with it. Therefore, a vital aspect of tapping into the potential that lies dormant within us so we can bloom in remarkable ways is to make the absolute most of the time we have by optimising each and every moment.

What is the goal? To minimise stress and maximise success. To be efficient and effective. To find and feel a sense of 'balance' in our days. To experience fulfilment and see progress in what counts. To squeeze every drop of magic and love from each second that passes by. And ultimately, it is to reach the end of our years here knowing without a shadow of a doubt that, yes, we have lived and loved and worked wholeheartedly and fulfilled our purpose. Albeit difficult at times, it is a worthy pursuit: to use our time well and to make sure it is truly ours.

You have a certain amount of bandwidth on a daily, weekly, and monthly basis. What does that mean? At any given moment, there is only so much that you can master. This bandwidth represents your mental ability, your physical energy, and your emotional capacity to *do* (to work, provide, create) and *process* (to digest, learn from, and gain wisdom in) your life experiences. Although we would very much like to be superhuman and do it 'all', it simply isn't possible. This leaves us in a position where we *must* find a way to make the best use of what time we have.

We make the most of our time by doing three powerful things. Firstly, by deciding what our true priorities in life are. By true priorities, I don't mean what task is the most pressing on your to-do list today. I mean your *life* priorities: what you are really here to achieve and experience, the true objective of your life and the legacy you wish to leave for the world around you.

These priorities become the true north for your life journey. They become the filter through which you make all decisions. They guide you to ignore, accept, or decline opportunities and advice. They tell you which way to go, which career path to follow, which relationship will complement your journey best. They are both the signpost and the destination.

They are the 'what' and 'why' for your existence, and ultimately, what gives your life its unique and profound meaning. Might your true priorities evolve over time as you evolve? Unquestionably. But without a sense of at least one true priority, your life will feel chaotic and random as opposed to a divine destiny unfolding with each day that passes.

With a clear focus on what counts, you can complete the next step: find a rhythm in your schedule and life that supports the achievement and fulfilment of these true priorities. This means scheduling in what matters. It means establishing regular time-blocks for your most important work. It means booking what you want and need to do for your goals into your diary. 'Someday' isn't in the calendar, so make sure that you have enough time and energy allocated to what matters.

Start by designing your long-term plan, then your mid-term plan, then create a short-term plan. Take the time to dream, to think, to strategise. Turn your dreams into plans, projects, and action steps. Then, book your dreams into your diary so that you can achieve them. Instead of complaining that you "never have enough time" and complaining about how time-poor you are, take control of your time. Make the most of the space and bandwidth you *do* have. Maximise your schedule.

The final step in optimising your time is incredibly important: it is to consistently focus your energy and attention on what matters. It is to recognise the precious nature of each moment of your life and protect it well. It is to say "No" with grace to those time-sucking commitments or people that pull us out of our optimum flow.

It is outsourcing the lower-value tasks that you struggle with to people who love doing them. It is also having the discipline to push projects back through time to allow you to maximise your bandwidth on higher priorities first. It is choosing what you would love and feel called to do as many times as often as possible.

If your time is all over the place, your energy will be, too. How can you achieve the extraordinary things you were born for if your schedule is scattered? How can you rise to the occasion or make profound breakthroughs or focus inwardly until the clarity 'pops' if your daily life is chaos? Jumping between 20 different tasks in a day and running around frantically rarely breeds greatness. Finding and maintaining your focus on the 20% of actions that creates 80% of the magic *does*.

Our effective time management goes out the window when we try to do it all or multitask our way to success. We overcommit our energy and stretch our already-limited attention span. We do the wrong things in the wrong order, or the wrong things at the wrong time, not allowing ample time for the work we need to complete. We leave too much room for distraction, where trivial things railroad our valuable attention and focus: get-rich-quick schemes, uninspiring drama, local gossip, unwarranted opinions, that friend who bombards your inbox seeking comfort or entertainment.

Your time IS your most valuable resource. It is the container for your entire existence, from birth to death. How do you want to use it? What would you *love* to do? What would you devote yourself, your energy, and your time to each day if you were to fulfil your dreams this year?

Make the commitment to get organised so that you can tap into the immense creative power of the present moment, which, by the way, is the only moment you will ever have. Assess and refine what your time is being spent on daily. Are you spending enough time on what you love? Are you doing what you live for? Are you progressing in the direction that lights you up? Simplify your life. Find your meaningful focal point. Structure your time around your heartfelt inspiring goals. Give yourself permission to make your time here truly extraordinary.

22
Wishful Thinking

"Action is the foundational key to all success."
Pablo Picasso

To dream about our future is an extraordinary thing. To close our outer eyes, open our heart, and imagine greater possibilities. To contemplate a future that is filled with all that we love. To picture what lights us up. To visualise what inspires us. To get clear on what we want for ourselves and the world around us.

We need dreams; they have phenomenal power to stir us from within to overcome adversity and to transform our life from the inside-out. But the fulfilment of those dreams is even more meaningful; to wake up in the morning looking forward to the day ahead, knowing that it is going to be another extraordinary day of doing what we love with people we care about.

It is when our dreams come true that we experience what I believe is the true beauty and wonder of life. We experience a deep respect for all that we have achieved, feel a deep love for ourselves for never giving up, and connect with an inspiring appreciation for the greater force that guides our path. We experience moments when our heart is open, where tears run down our face, and where we feel humbled because what we dream of has finally come true. We see and feel our own potential unleashed – and it is pure magic.

You want that for yourself. I want it for you, too. I wish it for all human beings. But what I also know is that our dreams don't manifest without taking action. In fact, they often require action that is far more courageous, consistent, and intensive than we may realise when we first start out on the path of designing our destiny.

In the beginning, we can be a little naïve. Amidst our enthusiasm, we can underestimate just how much we will be required to do to build and experience a fulfilling life and career. We can assume it will be easier or should happen quicker or be simpler than it really is. This causes us to either fall short of the work that is required to see our dreams to fruition… or give up completely.

We can doubt whether what we wish for is possible – but that doubt is *not* defeat, nor is it an omen to throw in the towel. It is often feedback to let us know that we are either lacking a plan or that we aren't taking action on the plan we set for ourselves. In other words, we are *thinking* about our dreams, but we aren't working on them daily.

This is wishful thinking: yearning for something we want without also putting in the effort to create it. It is expecting our dreams to manifest rapidly or for our path to be void of difficulty, wondering why creating the life we want is harder than we thought it might be. It is hoping for brighter days without realising that *we* have the power to turn on the sunshine. And yes, perhaps on a deeper level, we feel that our journey to the top should be free from obstacles because we feel we are born for great things (which we are).

The greatest expression of your purpose in life requires 50% action and 50% mindset: equal parts hard work and self-reflection; grunt and attraction; hard slog and support; outer effort and inner breakthrough. *That* is where the Law of Attraction is activated to its fullest power: when you firmly decide what you want, throw it out into the universe, and then apply your whole self to it. It can't and won't happen on meditation, prayers, hopes, or wishes alone.

When you become crystal clear on your dream, when you speak and act in alignment with what is inside your heart, and you work with a burning why at the forefront of your mind, you will become an extraordinary force. Life *will* open doors for you. You will attract miracles and unexpected support. Life wants to back those who are willing to get in the ring; those who apply themselves and who live *with* courage.

If you are not achieving what you would love or have not achieved what you dream yet, be honest with yourself: have you done everything you can to create it? Or have you accidentally slipped into the cycle of dreaming without doing? Are you receiving and contemplating ideas without following through on them? Are you receiving inspired guidance and hearing your calling from within but holding back on pursuing it?

Examine whether it's time for huge action or deep reflection. Ask yourself now, which one is it? What does your dream need from you the most right now? Is it a time of inner awakening to expand and clarify your vision? Or is a time of hustling needed to make sure that you do what you can with what you have?

It is entirely possible that you feel readier than ever to build your dreams, but you aren't sure what to do; that you know what you were born to do, but you have no idea how to get started. If so, ask yourself this: what *could* I do? Take out a pen and paper. Write down every action step you can think of that might help you get to where you want to be. Tap into your creative and strategic mind, listing as many ideas as you can.

Your list might include tasks like researching your industry, practising your skills, filming a video, writing content, networking, or hiring a mentor. Pick the one that feels right first… and then, act. Even if your first strategy doesn't work, you will at least be in motion. You will have created momentum, and this will help you to find your way forward to the strategy that *does* work. As you get into gear and go, the road will appear in front of you.

You were born to conquer and create, and when you apply yourself, a little or a lot each day, you *will* create the life you dream. Gone will be the doubts about whether you can do what you love because you will be *doing* it. By balancing action-taking with visualisation, you will break through. You will experience your power to move mountains and the mysterious ways in which life guides and blesses those individuals who are on an inspired mission.

Be one of the people who steps up. Who speaks their truth. Who tries new things. Who leads. Who expresses themselves openly. Who lives by example for others. Refuse to become another person who held back the magic within them, spending their entire life wishing but never reaching for more. Be one of the people who changes the world – and show others what is possible when we give our dreams our all.

23
RELATIONSHIP SACRIFICE

"Every person we meet in our life's journey, no matter how brief or long the encounter, takes a part of us with them and leaves a part of them with us, for eternity."

DR MARCIA BECHEREL
(TRANSLATED FROM PORTUGUESE)

Our relationships with the people in our life can affect whether we do or don't fulfil our true potential. They are personal, often emotional, and deeply meaningful. Therefore, how we navigate these relationships with friends, intimate partners, and family members is crucial. This does not relate to when the relationship encourages, drives, and fuels us towards our loftiest ambitions, but rather when we find ourselves holding onto that same relationship and sacrificing our dreams in the process.

How does this show up in our lives? Staying in a romantic relationship longer than we want to be there. Biting our tongue around family members instead of speaking our truth. Conforming to the norms of a friendship or social circle while making ourselves miserable. Being around a person with whom the conversation is depressing or draining. Or even being too afraid to share our original ideas or our latest work with a mentor because we fear they will shun us.

The cost of this is enormous. We end up aching in our own heart because we are repressing what we feel *born* to do – a pain that will only become greater as the years go by.

The fear of 'losing' someone can be significant in our journey. We sometimes fear that if we speak our truth or share our desires maybe that person won't understand us, will challenge us, disagree with us, or leave our life entirely. It is the belief or fear that reaching for or achieving what you want will cost you a connection with someone you care for – or even someone you have become dependent on for financial support, for a sense of safety, for conversation, for guidance, or for approval.

And you know what? Maybe it's true. Maybe as you break out and change your life radically, your friends won't understand you and will reject you from their social circle. Or maybe your partner won't be in favour of your new career path or business, and it will be the cause of your break-up. Or maybe a family member won't understand your new perspective on life, your relationship choices, your decision to live a non-traditional life. And perhaps you will go through a grief phase at the same time you go through a growth phase.

But if that is true, then it begs this question: if you *do* part ways with a person because you went after your dreams, was that relationship as authentic, deep, and meaningful as you originally thought? Or were you holding back all that time for a connection that may have fit you in the past but won't fit you in the future – and the truth is that you have outgrown it?

I personally want to fill my life with only the kind of relationships where we can fly, break through, break down, and grow on the path of fulfilling our destiny – no hesitations. Where we can discuss what truly matters, the exquisite depths of life, not just the shallows. Where we feel a deep sense of reverence and respect for one another and appreciate our uniqueness, rather than trying to be the same.

If those people with whom I can be authentic are family, great. If they aren't, that's okay. I have ended relationships, drifted away from relatives, and faded out numerous friendships over the years in an effort to be true to myself. Was it easy? No. Sometimes breaking it off or realising that the relationship had run its course was stressful, emotional, or heart-wrenching.

But the way I make peace with the necessary endings that I know are in my best interest is not with bitterness or anger like we can sometimes tend to do, but rather to celebrate and express gratitude for what the partnership or connection brought to my life and to let go with grace. It is to set us both free with love while trusting in the bigger order of life.

And what about family? The people without whom we wouldn't be here and whom we have spent so much time with? What do we do if they misunderstand or judge us? Although I have not experienced rejection from family members personally, my intuition is to do whatever you can to move on with your life while keeping love in your heart for your relatives. Send them respect, appreciation, gratitude, and well wishes for their journey – and live with a clear conscience for the choices you have made.

What if you want to pull away and be the one who withdraws from the family? Do what feels right. See them on your terms. As you grow older, you will probably appreciate them more – parents, siblings – and the love will grow. It doesn't mean you have to visit or communicate with them on a regular basis; that's up to you. Just make sure you don't have regrets later in your journey.

My view on family relationships is that each person doing well, doing what they love, and being their true, authentic self is what counts the most. That is what I am the most interested in: a deeply fulfilling life for each one of us. Together or apart, that is where the love is the deepest. I don't expect my family to be there for me and my family don't expect me to be there for them. The appreciation is there, and we know it. We just want the best for each other.

This might sound strange because maybe it's not the way you were raised or perhaps you have an entirely different desire for your family life or a varied understanding of what family is – and that's okay. It's simply about choosing your authentic path with all of the relationships in your life, personal and professional.

Life is bittersweet. On your journey, it is inevitable that you *will* drift away from and drift towards people, whether they be friends, partners, or family members. It's natural and necessary. We are here to connect and love – YES – and we are also here each with an individual path of purpose to fulfil: a calling that yearns to be pursued, experienced, and fulfilled. The future has many great adventures in store for us all, and it would be a shame if we missed out on those because we were afraid that setting sail for our dreams would cost us a relationship with a certain person.

Relationship Sacrifice

In times when we have become distant from those we love, whom we are related to, or those whom we once cared for, it helps to remember that there are eight billion people on this planet, and you won't ever be alone (unless you choose it that way). Your tribe ARE out there. The perfect partner is out there. Your soul family are waiting. And you will find each other. Have faith in that.

24
Extreme Adversity

"One day, in retrospect, the years of struggle will strike you as the most beautiful."

Sigmund Freud

It's possible that you have faced a long line of struggles in your journey and that you feel bruised and worn out to the point that fulfilling your dreams seems like it will never happen for you. Perhaps you feel defeated by the events of your life and have no idea how you could ever overcome your obstacles and thrive, where extreme adversity seems to have gotten the better of you.

I cannot speak directly to this from my personal journey, as I would not say that my own life has been riddled with chaos and difficulty, but what I do know is this: this world is filled with courageous people who have been through hell and back, who have been tried and tested in unimaginable ways, and who, despite their difficulties, have gone on to do awe-inspiring things in this world.

In fact, this is true of many of the world's leaders and legends, that they were beaten up and wrung out before breaking through. What may have initially seemed hard or cold became the springboard for their success. Their unbearable circumstances gave rise to their unlikely yet God-given and highly inspiring achievements.

The people's stories I have heard on my journey follow similar themes: of beating the impossible odds to make it, of finding their way through to the other side, of breaking open and discovering their fight to *live*. From bouncing back after injury to writing a book at 81 after the death of a son to losing a child mid-pregnancy, the people I've met on my path have touched me in extraordinary ways. These remarkable individuals stir our indestructible spirit and remind us that there *is* light at the end of the tunnel.

I also know that pain can drive us to extraordinary lengths. The angst, the heartache, the stress we experience can push us from a place deep within to realise what matters, to find a new way forwards, and to find the strength we didn't know we had – to carry on, to turn it around, to recover, to make the most of our life. Sometimes we *need* the struggle in order to succeed (and we wouldn't without it).

If I had not been bullied and socially excluded at school, would I have become a writer? If I had not felt so deeply misunderstood and overwhelmed by my own emotions, would I have ever turned to the page? If I had never felt small, shy, or insignificant, would I have discovered my lifelong fascination for human potential or fallen in love with self-development?

Sometimes the power beyond us has a way of guiding us to where we were always meant to be and shaping us into who we were always meant to become. Sometimes what hurts us the most shapes in us exactly the qualities we need to fulfil our destiny on Earth. Sometimes the challenging times become our richest source of growth. The shadows shape us, and it is often in the heart of the fight when we discover our light. Therefore, the very fire that once burned us can become the very same flames that transform us so we can rise out of the ashes like the Phoenix.

We must remember that we are far tougher than we think and far more resilient than we realise. We often have untapped power to defeat obstacles, to heal on a deep level, to build something astonishing out of nothing. So, how do we do it? How do we turn our greatest obstacles into our greatest advantages?

We look right into the heart of the pain and seek the beauty until it opens our heart. We ask ourselves: what miracle is this creating? What new path am I being set on? What is the healing, the blessing, the silver lining here? Why was this challenge required? What is this experience trying to give me? What qualities is this developing in me? Who was or is the divine trying to raise me to be?

We relinquish expectations on life to be easy or peaceful or a flow experience 24 hours a day. We become wiser. We focus our attention instead on the growth, the depth, the wisdom, and the love – and understand the divine reason why this event occurred. It is when we do this that our mind clears, our heart opens, and we find the freedom we yearned for all along.

We cannot meet our destiny and experience the endless blessings that life has in store for us by cowering in the shadows of our difficulties, our wounds, our sorrow. Rather, it is only in leaning in courageously to that which stings where our obstacles can unlock our greatness. It is often our toughest struggles that push us to do what we wanted to do all along (but were hesitating about) and to become who we wanted to be all along – and *that* is the gift in our trials and tribulations, our down days, our rock-bottom moments. They nudge and push us forwards, so that we take a leap of faith and fly.

Ask yourself, what is the alternative to a life of adversity? Is it a life of comfort? Of pure ease? An empty existence where you never leave your own comfort zone much less discover what you are made of? Would you truly want that? And would you have grown so exponentially if your life had not panned out the way it did?

Embrace this divine truth that this IS the life you were meant to have. You came onto this planet armed with every dream, wish, and purpose to fulfil, and each one of your experiences – brutal or gentle, excruciating or elevating – has been preparing, guiding, and empowering you to do exactly that.

Have faith in the greater plan for your life and trust each step of your journey. Trust the divine to guide you. Seek the beauty and infinite possibility in every moment. Let life grow you but not make you scared, hard, or bitter. There IS a way through whatever you face today. It happens one step, one answer, one quiet whisper from your soul, and one nudge from your heart at a time.

You may have been challenged – okay, you may have been pushed to edges you didn't even know you had – but these adversities were not placed in your life to defeat you. They are not a personal attack on you. We all have our own demons to wrestle with and our own pain to surmount, no exceptions.

Regardless of what this looks like for you, remember that how your story pans out depends on what you, as the main character of it all, do with that struggle. Will you be defeated? Or will you *get* what life was trying to achieve by testing you and rise to your glory?

25
GIVING UP EARLY

"The simple difference between people who achieve their dreams and those that don't is two things: the courage to start and the discipline to keep going."

BILL ACKMAN

Are you ready to acknowledge an uncomfortable yet vital truth? Your dreams and goals are going to require *far* more patience and persistence than you might realise – and any version of short-term immediate gratification of wanting pleasure and rewards now can undermine your long-term sustainable fulfilment. Simply put, giving up early is where you walk away from your dreams before they've had a chance to manifest or where you stop working on your goals before you have reached the milestone.

My client Ralph Anania once referred to our impatience in life as 'click and collect' mentality – where we want what we want, and we want it *now*. I know from my own journey and from studying the lives of the greats (people who have done outstanding things in this world) that trying to have what we want immediately without both the work and time required to achieve it ultimately ends up hurting us later on.

In other words, our short-term focus can cost us our dreams. Our unwillingness to be patient, sit still, and *let* things happen as well as get active, persist, and *make* them happen can limit what we achieve in all areas of our life, from health and wealth, to career and our personal relationships.

Missing steps in the process, rushing your way through a project, trying to cut corners, deciding that things won't work out before they can, missing vital details in the hurry, ruling yourself out of the game, and skipping out on a plan before it has had a chance to work: these are some of the many ways in which we weigh our dreams down with impatience.

What causes this lack of necessary patience and persistence? It could certainly be a side-effect of our modern-day world, where so much is available almost instantly – and at our fingertips, no less. Perhaps our brains, emotions, and bodies have been wired for instant reward, and so it becomes more difficult to think, long-term about our goals, our plans, our lives. Doing this takes effort and energy, silence and stillness, discipline and focus, time and patience, faith and trust. We can't simply press a button to get the clarity we need. We must reflect, think, contemplate, and feel to achieve that.

Or perhaps our tendency to give up early is rooted in something else entirely, namely that we had unrealistic expectations about what was involved in the achievement of what we desire. Perhaps we didn't realise how difficult our path of purpose was going to be or what challenges we would experience along the way. Maybe we faced a long line of unexpected obstacles once we got going. All of these can be reasons for people to feel disheartened or even give up on what their heart aches for.

Have you ever heard the expression that you might be just one breakthrough away from your big break? It's true. But what is also true is that you could be five, ten, or fifty breakthroughs away from that break you have been waiting for. If that is the case, isn't it still worth it to push forwards and keep at it? Or are you going to tap out early simply because more growth is required for you to blast into the stratosphere?

This is where patience and persistence are needed in great measures, to make damn well sure that you *do* achieve your dreams here. That you become exactly who you were born to be and express what you feel and explore what you think and make waves in this world. That you break through every single invisible barrier that holds you back – and make your mark on humanity.

If this is what is inside your heart, you will stick with it. You won't walk away, because you don't want to. No matter how tough the terrain, you will push forwards. You will drive right through the ruts you find yourself in, with your eyes focused firmly on the road in front of you. And you won't allow a setback or a little self-doubt stop you, because this is your DREAM. It is what you were born for. Made for. Designed for. It is your destiny – and you feel it down to the tips of your fingers and toes. You know this path is yours. It's not a sprint. It's a marathon. It's the journey of your life.

So, what if you demonstrated patience towards yourself and *allowed* yourself to grow? What if you gave yourself more time and worked *with* yourself in all that you are achieving, feeling, and facing? What if you remembered that most great things take time to flourish?

What if you loved yourself so deeply that you were willing to see things through to the end, even when you have to be patient while your dreams take root and grow? What if you harnessed your persistence? What if you refused to give up when things get difficult or when the outcome you want seems out of reach and like it will never happen?

Maybe you will need to work a part-time job while you build your business. Maybe you will need more downtime than you realised while working on your goals incrementally. Maybe the process will be tougher, trickier, or more complicated than you hoped. Maybe those refinements, changes, and foundations will take longer to implement than you thought. None of these are reasons to quit the dream inside your heart.

It takes maturity to be patient and wisdom to realise when you are at risk of stopping before the finish line. It means first, noticing when we are approaching our work with a hurried energy or recognising when we are tapping out before the win. And then, it is digging deep within ourselves to find the determination required to move forwards. To put the master plan in motion, build momentum, and experience the results that we dream of.

Don't let giving up early be the cause of your unfulfilled dreams or your untapped potential. Rome wasn't built in a day – and the life you dream of won't be either. It's a fact. You are here for a lifetime, and it will all be worth the patience and persistence required for you to find your purpose, figure out what you want, discover who you are, grow the career you want, establish a thriving business, master your relationships, get rich, heal yourself, and *live* the way you dream.

26
VICTIM MENTALITY

"There are only two kinds of people. Those who believe that they are a victim of the world and those who understand that they are the world."

ALAN WATTS

Living life with a victim mentality is often recognisable by the behaviour of blaming someone else, anyone else, for our own pain, difficulty, or problems. It is placing responsibility for the suffering and pain we personally have experienced onto someone else while simultaneously ignoring and denying our role and power to change, cause, and create situations. It is the 'poor me' story. *Why do bad things always happen to me? I am the way I am because that evil person did that to me when I was young. It's the fault of the government, my ex-partners, family, or my boss that I can't live the life that I want.*

Without question, this is *extremely* detrimental to the fulfilment of one's potential. In fact, I would even go as far as to say that running a victim mentality and a greatness mentality at the same time is impossible. How can you lead your life courageously while feeling wounded by the people and events you encounter? How can you build wealth or health let alone a thriving career or a world-touching legacy if you feel everything that goes wrong is someone else's fault? The two simply don't mix.

Believing that you are a victim in any way will cause you to feel weak, frustrated, and powerless, and any sympathy you receive from anyone who also feels wounded won't outweigh the desire within you to master your own life. But what I want to explore here is not so much why victimhood mentality cost us our dreams, but rather what causes it.

In my experience, victim mentality is underpinned by two things. The first one is an abdication of our personal responsibility in the circumstances and situations we experience and thus a dis-ownership, denial, and repression of our personal power. The second is an emotional attachment and addiction to the support we receive by telling and retelling a sob story to the world around us about how disadvantaged or damaged we are because of what 'they' said or did, or because of what happened in the past. Together, these drain our energy and breed disempowerment.

For some people, victim mentality colours their entire life. For others – most of us, I hope – it affects smaller aspects of our life: areas where we haven't created what we want yet, where we lack an action plan, where we are avoiding responsibility, or where we feel weak and stressed instead of powerful.

Assess yourself now. Where have you not yet sat in the driver's seat? Where are you allowing others to run the show when you know it's on you? Where are you settling for less because you haven't asked for what you want yet? Where are you being mistreated and tolerating situations that irk you because you haven't spoken up yet? Regardless of the areas where we could change our victim story, healing it is one of the greatest gifts we can give ourselves: to shift the entire narrative of our inner self and thus our entire life from wounded to warrior.

To dissolve victim mentality, we must recognise our ability to create the life we want. We must realise that we *can* change our own fortune. We are not voiceless or powerless by any means. We *can* break the patterns that don't work for us anymore and we *can* transcend our adversities.

The beautiful irony of victim mentality is that by stepping into our power, we attract fewer situations that cause us to feel like a victim. It is a cosmic comedy that when we avoid taking responsibility on all levels, we attract difficulty, but, when we lean *in* ready to grow, life lifts us up. THIS is what enables us to manifest the life we desire.

There are three spiritual truths to embrace to break out of victim mentality in every area of your life. The first is that you are continually co-creating your life with God, the higher power, and the divine order. The second is that because of this, you *put* yourself in many of the circumstances, situations, and dynamics that you face in life – and there is enormous power in recognising this. And thirdly is that you *need* each thing you encounter on your path, regardless of how challenging it was or is. It is never any other way; we just either don't see it or we don't want to see it, and this is what causes victim mentality.

Are these truths difficult to adopt? Yes. But embracing them *will* change your destiny in this world. When you reach the stage where you would prefer that people respect you for your accomplishments, not pity you for your hardships nor comfort you for your unfulfilled dreams, you will *rise*. Hear me roar.

No matter what is occurring right now or where you find yourself in this moment, there is a next step you can take, a lesson to learn, a wisdom to gain, and a way to grow through this. So, vow to yourself right now to never be a victim or to feel wounded by something that you haven't yet stepped in to change. If you don't like a part of your life, either change it or change your feelings around it. Either way, don't allow circumstances to defeat the vision in your soul.

Speak up. Fight for it. Be proactive. Don't expect others to please you or read your mind. Respect yourself. Be clear in your communication, your requests, your boundaries. Be clear on consequences and the ripple effect of your actions. You CAN do this. You can live alone. Grow a business. Earn enough. Build wealth. You are not small or insignificant and you don't have to be a doormat for the world around you.

Sometimes when we feel defeated or downtrodden or ripped off or betrayed, it helps to remember that there are many people who face far greater adversities than we do and who are doing far more with their life than most would under the same circumstances. These people are an inspiration. They are a reminder to never allow the trivial to undermine what is meaningful in our lives. The lesson here is that it truly is not what we encounter that determines the end of our story: it's on us to define and decide that. We hold the power.

Accepting and openly embracing this journey of owning your power and empowering your life is liberating. *This* is what enables us to lead our lives. To overcome obstacles with grace and speed. To never feel completely powerless or helpless, no matter how hopeless things may seem. It is what enables us to get past our pain and discover just how much we are capable of. It empowers us to look for the blessings in the crisis and to turn humble beginnings into great endings.

27
Disempowerment

"This is your world. Shape it or someone else will."

Natalie Setareh

It is impossible to create the life that you dream of without tapping into and expressing the power within you. Your external world mirrors the state of your internal world, intimately, precisely, and 24 hours a day. This means that if you are not in the driver's seat of your own life, you will find it incredibly difficult to steer yourself in the direction you want to go.

Tapping into your personal power means being dedicated to mastery in the many aspects of your life, from your physical health to your career path to your relationships to your financial wealth. It means investing in yourself and your future. It is an ongoing commitment and steadfast devotion to living an authentic and enriched existence.

When we ignore our need for growth, we create shadows in our life. These become those stressful areas where we tend to feel highly emotional, lost, or stressed. Instead of leading the charge and upgrading aspects of ourselves and our lives, we avoid facing the growth and the challenge. We remain caught in the fight for survival, never quite fulfilling our own desire for personal expansion and self-actualisation.

This can certainly lead to us feeling like a victim of our circumstances, as we explored in the previous topic. What I have often noticed is that when we don't empower ourselves, we can also attract even more challenges, which I believe are life's attempts to toughen us up for the mission that we were born for. In a nutshell, either you are going to pick the challenge and toughen yourself up, or life will do it for you.

There are enormous gifts in being proactive about your empowerment, in seeking the education, training, and breakthroughs that can make the difference for you. It is the most extraordinary process, transforming and empowering ourselves and our lives. When we apply ourselves and show up, willing to learn and grow, magic happens.

We attract miracles, higher quality people are drawn towards us, and opportunities are offered to us. We discover who we are and everything that we have to offer, and we experience everything that life has to offer us in return. We feel a greater sense of our own destiny as we work on ourselves and our life as the greatest project of all.

This is where and how we begin to achieve holistic fulfilment and success. This means that instead of choosing between your career or your family, you experience fulfilment in both. You no longer need to sacrifice your health for your business, your wealth for your relationship, your relationship for your career, or anything that matters to you – because you are empowering all areas, trusting that they will coexist in innate harmony… that you can truly 'have it all'.

I believe with certainty and know from experience that it is 100% possible to have a life that feels meaningful every day. You don't have to give up on that vision. It is just important to remember that the price we pay for achieving that life is to own and use our power. If we continue to deny, delay, distort, or disown our power, we will likely undermine the very goals that we cannot go a day without thinking about.

As you actively empower yourself, you compound the value that lies dormant inside you. As you refine your skills, learn, heal your emotions, and do what you know must be done for you to achieve what you yearn for, you elevate yourself and your life. You *become* the package – personally and professionally – and the world *will* respond to you differently as a result, because you are *empowered*.

Yes, you are deeply worthy of your dreams right now. I have no doubt about that. But imagine yourself and the life you could be living if you were five times more powerful. Imagine yourself more accomplished in your career, your work, your business. Imagine yourself earning ten times the amount you are today. Imagine your confidence when your body transformation is complete. Imagine how whole and complete you will feel with unconditional love flowing through your personal relationships. THAT is a 'you' that you deserve to be – and you already have the ingredients and raw power within you to achieve it.

Yes, you will still experience challenge and pain in life because it is part of life, on every level of accomplishment and existence. But even when it shows up, you will handle it differently. The more empowered expression of you will *know* exactly what to do, who to reach out to, and which wisdom will help you achieve the outcome you want. Stumbling blocks will become stepping stones overnight.

How do you empower yourself? Make a plan for your life. Set up action steps for yourself in every area so you know what you are working on now and next. Create a rolling business plan as well as a personal development plan.

What would you love to transform? What would you love to learn? What isn't working right now? Which habits need to go? What would you like to remove or introduce? Where are you less empowered than what you want and what you know you could be?

It is time to claim this more empowered 'you' for yourself. The 'you' who refuses to be defeated, no matter how broken apart or sad or stressed you might feel at times on your journey. The 'you' that seeks to expand, evolve, and experience all that life has to offer. The 'you' that you were born to be and that life is and has been shaping you to be.

No more telling yourself disempowering stories about why you cannot do what you want or why you will not achieve your dreams. It is time to change your internal dialogue and do what you can to empower yourself to manifest what you love and live this life on your terms.

28

AGEISM

"Dreams don't have timelines, deadlines, and aren't always in straight lines."

JASON REYNOLDS

It's time to talk about age – or more specifically, the belief that you are either too young or too old to pursue your dreams. This idea is incredibly limiting, so let's reframe it. Your biological age is nothing more than a mere measure of your time here. And while it can provide you with some useful parameters for health and life, let it not be a reason to hold back from what you love to do nor the reason why you can't unleash the potential within you.

If you think you are too young to pursue your destiny inside your heart, search online for the fashion designer Max Alexander. Max began designing clothes at the early age of 4. By age 8, he had launched a career and a global brand in the fashion industry. If you watch any video of Max in his flow, it is clear to see that this talented young man was simply born to create a fashion legacy.

Or reflect on my journey, where I began writing as a child, fell in love with spirituality by age 16, wrote my first self-help book at 18 while studying full-time at university, and became self-employed by age 19. By the time I hit adulthood, I knew what I wanted to do with my life and in the world, and after overcoming near-suicidal depression, I got on my way. I started early with my writing and speaking, built a career, and was living my dreams by the time I was 21 years old – and I haven't stopped since.

If you think you are too old to pursue your dreams, listen to the story of my mother, fondly known by many as Mama Rae. Inspired by all things wellness and nourishment, Mama Rae wrote, published, and launched her first book, *Vital & Alive at 75* on her 75th birthday. The book shares her powerful wisdom on eating and living well. It is a true reflection of the way she lives her life, choosing how she wants to 'age' rather than being defined by the norms of the world.

Mama Rae believes that our potential is limitless and that our dreams are timeless. As she said to me, "I'm not going to stop until I've done it." Although I know she sometimes worries that she could still be doing more, I see the difference that she makes in people's lives, including mine, and I know in my heart that her legacy is being left in this world every single day. She is a true inspiration to *all* people of any age.

Or read the story of Louise Hay, visionary of the global book publishing empire Hay House, who founded the company in her 60s. Or remember that Frank Lloyd Wright, one of the world's most significant architects, completed one third of his life's work between the ages of 80 and 92. There is an endless list of legends who made their breakthrough after the age of 50 or 60 – and you could be one of them.

At any stage in your life, your age is not a measure of your potential nor a cap on your dreams nor a reason why you cannot or will not succeed. So, use it as a starting block not a stopping point. Instead of viewing it as a limitation, use it as an inspiration. Have it be the reason you *can*, not the reason you can't. However old you are today is just a detail in the big picture, and it does not have to define your story nor dictate what you do with the rest of your years.

Draw encouragement from those inspiring individuals who care far more about their own path than what others think of their age. Who are too deeply immersed in their life's work to mind mind how old they are. Who do what they can with what they have and where they're at in their journey. Who are blazing trails and showing the rest of us that age truly is just a number, especially when it comes to chasing and living our dreams.

Those who are giving it their all while they are young show us that we are ready NOW. They teach us to step up before we feel ready. That it is okay to try different things until we find our purpose. That it is when we get *in* the ring that we develop our mastery. That there is never a 'right moment' to start, because this moment right here is the only moment we ever have. Those who are in the later years of their life and pursuing what they feel inspired to do teach us that time is precious. They show us that it is never too late to turn it around and that growing older doesn't mean giving up on our goals, our purpose, or our life's work.

Whether young or old, the message is the same: do it now. Live now. Carpe diem. Seize the day. Don't wait. Don't hesitate any longer, and don't ever use the age of your physical body to stop you from what inspires you or an excuse as to why your dreams are still locked up inside your heart. Ask yourself, when *is* the right time to chase one's dreams? When we're a teenager? When we've retired from a job we worked in our whole life? When we're a child? When our children leave home? The *only* time is today.

Maybe the divine has a plan for you to do it all by age 20 or to have three careers in one life or to collect experiences in the first half of your life and then spend the second half of your life sharing your wisdom. However, your unique journey here unfolds, *trust* in the greater plan for your life and continue to pray for the courage to act upon what is inside your heart.

Break out of the societal norms of what you think should or could be done by someone your age. Who says that all young people need a college degree? Or to get married in their 20s? Or have kids before 35 (or at all)? Or work a job for 40 years? Or retire at 60 instead of 30? Those ideas of 'normal' might seem comforting, but they might run a completely different course from your destiny, your journey, your story. That's the thing about unleashing your potential: YOU are the one who decides what your timeline looks like and when is the right time to do it.

My advice is to be present with where and who you are in this sacred moment. Ask yourself what is next for you in your life. Ask yourself what your dream is, what you feel moved to do next, what your next creation will be. Then get busy living. Don't miss this precious moment of being 12 or 24 or 45 or 72 or 91. It's your stage, so get out there and dance.

29
One-Dimensional Living

"I fall in love every day. With new songs, dogs, scents, pieces of art, illusions, five-minute conversations, a sunset in my rearview mirror, a story. A written note. A daydream. What a pleasure it is.
To know gravity."

Victoria Erickson

When I was a little girl, around the age of three or four, my mother (Mama Rae, as I shared in the previous chapter) used to sit in the garden in the mornings with my sister Cassie and me. While we were waiting for the sun to rise, we would look around us at all the plants and bugs. As the sun came up, we watched the poppies. When the rays of light touched the flowers, the outside casing of the poppy would slowly pop off and the flower would open to reveal all its beauty. To Mama Rae's recollection, we were mesmerised by the experience.

This and many other similar experiences in my childhood are just one of the reasons that my mum was and is a significant blessing in my life. She was deeply present with me when I was a child and often took time to slow down and teach both my sister and me about the world around us. She pointed to the magic so that I could see it and then find it on my own as an adult.

One-Dimensional Living

She taught me to live with awe – to look for the beauty in the moment, to be curious, to want to *know* and *see* and *feel* – and I will forever be grateful for her influence. It set me on a lifelong journey of seeking magic, mystery, and depth. It inspired me to open my eyes and my heart and look at the world around me with curiosity and wonder, which has awakened me to a life far beyond what I refer to as one-dimensional living.

One-dimensional living is where we become caught up in routine and in our habits. Our life becomes a little monotonous, like Groundhog Day. We become all work and no play. Life can turn to black and white instead of being high-definition colour. We become too structured with our approach to work.

Without realising it, we try to force, plan, control, and predict each moment of our life. We spend every day in the same environments with the same people doing the same tasks. We wake up with the same alarm every day, eat the same foods, go to the same places, and stay where we are for years on end.

Even if we are working towards our dreams and progressing towards goals we care about in the process, if we do the same thing over and over for too long, we can end up feeling empty, uninspired, and flat. We can disconnect from our vision, forget the bigger picture of our life, and lose touch with the awe that makes life worth living.

Remember the freedom and spontaneity of being a teenager? Of starting the day with no expectation of where we might end up upon sundown? Of being OPEN and READY for life to happen and greeting each moment without attachment? *This* is what we so often need more of as adults: to approach our life and every moment of it as an adventure. To remember that we were born from nothing and we will return to nothing, and that there are many levels and layers to life that are worth experiencing.

How do we tap into multidimensional living so that we can feel alive and awake again? We get out of the ordinary, the usual, the norm. We book that trip, take that leap of faith, sign ourselves up for that program, and let our heart lead us. We let new people and new energy appear in our lives. That is how we enrich our reality and rediscover the fire within us.

Standing on the Great Wall of China, waking up in Bali, staying in my favourite hotels, writing in London, and living in several countries were all moments that have made my life so sweet. So touching. So precious. But these moments of awe, where we are living the life we dream of, don't have to cost a fortune. They are available to us every day.

It's putting on a nice frock. It's walking barefoot in the grass. It's looking up at the sky. It's a live concert. A busker in the street. A heart-to-heart conversation. Eating a fresh mango. A moment of healing, relaxation, humour, intimacy, stillness. Dancing until our feet hurt. Watching the sun go down over the water. It is anything that enlivens your senses and opens your mind, that which moves the body and touches the heart. That which invites spontaneity, sweetness, spirituality, and synchronicity into your daily life.

I believe in the very core of my heart that for you to truly thrive, you must open yourself to these experiences and to life itself. Your time here is powerful, beautiful, and deep – and if you become *too* serious or *too* focused on work to the exclusion of all else, you might never discover the true meaning of why you are here – nor the truth of who you are. It is in breaking our usual pattern from time to time that we find new insight, learn new things, and feel what is deep underneath the surface so we can heal and release it.

New experiences. Spiritual awakening. Moments of magic. Yes, sensory pleasures. We *need* these the same way that we need our purpose: to ignite us and inspire us, to move us from deep within to do our best, to go our furthest, to not settle for less than our heart desires. Your purpose gives you direction for your short journey here… and your experiences are what make that journey exquisite.

These open-hearted moments of wonder and awe are what make life truly, truly worth it; when we discover, rediscover, feel, and fall in love with life, with the unknown, with the simple things. When we soften, open, and surrender to the present moment and the mystery. They are the moments when you *know* in your heart that you are living the extraordinary life you desire.

They blow the cobwebs and the stiffness out of our body and mind. They lighten us up and enlighten our lives. They remind us to play. To reward ourselves for our efforts. To cry our heart out when we finally break through and to let the tears of love for the bittersweetness of life stream down our face. To stand outside in the storm and let the rain wash over us. To allow ourselves to be sweetly, imperfectly human: our true, raw, wild, untamed self. Living fully and free to be ourselves.

30
DIGITAL DROWNING

"Sometimes you just have to unplug from everything to find yourself again."

ROBIN LEE

Tech, tech, tech, and more tech. It has become so ingrained in the way we live that it is nearly impossible to avoid it. It wouldn't be a stretch to say that most people spend the majority of their day with a screen in front of their face, fixated on notifications and overstimulated by endless amounts of digital information. It is a far cry from how life used to be just a few short decades ago.

We live our lives on it, connect with our friends through it, document our memories with it, use it for work, for wealth, for learning, for entertainment, and for creation. Apps, scheduling software, online platforms, and online media have now seemingly become essential to our very existence. The question is, are we running it, or is it running us?

Of all our habits surrounding and our relationship with technology, social media use – and overuse, in particular – requires the most careful examination. The platforms are designed to hook us, engage us, entertain us, and intrigue us. And it works. Of course, it provides a service to our lives that is, in some ways, immeasurably valuable.

It enables us to connect, to express ourselves, to share who we are and what we believe in, to travel the world virtually. The emergence of social media has enabled us to transcend the limits of time and location to form new personal and professional relationships.

The problem is when we spend so much time browsing or scrolling that we lose what is often critical traction time on our own goals. Or we become overly wound up from indulging in excessive screen time. Or we view the highlight reel from a perfect stranger's life and hide in the shadows of it. Or we feel as though we can't live without technology; that we wouldn't know who we are or what to do without it.

The other danger is when we become so dependent on it that we feel lost and lonely the second we go offline. Or we have filled our life with so many digital platforms, software, and contraptions that we have lost touch with what is wholesome. Or we are so caught up in showing the world our own highlight reel, that we feel pressure to be 'on' or polished or perfect all the time to keep people watching, creating a filtered life where we project an image of ourselves that isn't authentic.

From a mental, emotional, and spiritual perspective, it is an unhealthy pattern to get caught up in: when we start to enjoy our online life more than we enjoy our offline life. It is here where we become disconnected from all of those nourishing, meaningful, and inspiring experiences that we must be offline to have.

Like sitting with the people that you love around a campfire talking about life. Deep, undisturbed conversation with a friend. Walking in nature, breathing in the fresh air, swimming in the ocean. Dropping into meditation and finding God. Spiritual awakenings. Sunsets and sunrises. Developing your relationship with yourself. Connected and heart-opening lovemaking. Creativity on high. Cuddling your dog. Meeting people in person rather than through a screen.

What are you looking for when you scroll the feed or lose yourself in a YouTube vortex? How do you feel as your thumb flicks mindlessly through the feed of whatever platforms you frequent? What feeling are you searching for? My experience is that what we find in 'the feed' rarely changes our life. In fact, more often than not, it distracts us from our life.

Those answers you yearn for, the clarity you seek, the breakthrough you crave: it can rarely be discovered by watching someone else's life, stalking that person's profile, or by spending every waking minute of your life plugged into a virtual world. In fact, they often happen when we are nowhere near a screen: when we are unplugged from tech and plugged into something far more powerful. Our higher mind. Our heart. Our inner wisdom.

They occur when we give our eyes a break from the glare of the screen and find the glow of our soul instead. What we will find there is far more enriching and life-changing. It is profoundly powerful and much-needed – for all aspects of our wellness – and yet it is increasingly rare.

Here is a sidenote about the impact of extensive use of technology on your body. Did you know that when you watch a screen while eating, you are more likely to overeat? This is because you are distracted and therefore don't sense when leptin (the hormone that lets you know that you are full) has been triggered.

Are you also aware that staring at a screen for hours on end prohibits the production of melatonin in your body, the hormone that helps you go to sleep? And did you know that every time you receive a notification on your social media or your inbox, it triggers a hit of dopamine in your body? These scary facts explain why and how an overuse of screen time can not only drain our energy but damage our body in the long run.

Besides the effect that screentime has on our eyesight and several important functions and rhythms in the body, there are many other ramifications on our health of living our life online. We did not come from this space. We were born to live outside and run through the fields, to bathe in the streams, to be one with nature, and to look up at the sky. And so, it is crucial, if for no other reason than for our vitality and longevity, to be mindful of how we interact with our tech.

What is your relationship with technology like right now? How are you interacting with and in the digital world? How much time do you spend at your desk or with your phone in your hand? Is it healthy? Helpful? Inspiring? Are you utilising technology well or using it to fill an empty void in your day?

Are you checking your messages, your emails, your inboxes, your notifications *too* often? Is it consuming you? What could you do with more offline time, away from an endless stream of notifications and 'ding ding'? Is it time for a digital detox, to live more of your life in flight mode?

The rejuvenation and the solace that will automatically start flooding into your life when you unplug is unparalleled, extraordinary, and exquisite – and you *need* it. In even one hour of offline time, you will start to feel centred, calmer, and present. You will find that sense of balance that you have lost touch with. Answers and insights will appear. You will start to feel like yourself again. So, give that to yourself, that quality offline time for your mind, body, and soul.

Yes, use technology as a tool to master your life and create your work in the world, but don't be so plugged into your devices that you never plug into your own soul. Because that is where you will find the answers you need and be able to do the work that truly matters, the work that changes the world and creates the life you dream of.

31
DODGING DISCOMFORT

"Character cannot be developed in ease and quiet. Only through experience of trial and suffering can the soul be strengthened, vision cleared, ambition inspired, and success achieved."

HELEN KELLER

It is human instinct to want the easy path, the path of least resistance, to achieve our goals in life. However, as much as we may try to avoid challenge, it is inevitable. As you have already discovered, life has no shortage of obstacles. They just keep coming in every stage of our journey.

Therefore, you have two options: you can be defeated by your difficulties, or you can master them. If you lean into growth, you unleash your power and potential. But if you dodge, delay, or ignore your own evolution, you will attract even more challenges that are designed to wake you up and empower you.

The following are all ways in which we try to dodge the discomfort that would help us achieve our dreams. We avoid facing or addressing our problems. We want to achieve our goals quickly without difficulty or delay. We yearn for someone else to do the hard work for us. We delay the complex yet essential tasks that produce results. We wear rose-coloured glasses, holding onto fantasies and wanting life to be easy.

Then, we wonder why our life isn't flowing and why we aren't getting to where we want to go. We cling to comfort instead of seeking a worthy challenge, an inspired mission, and a meaningful problem to solve. This emotional immaturity costs us greatly: wisdom, self-discovery, expansion – even the very life that we dream of. As Mitch Orowitz stated powerfully, "If we don't grow through friction, we remain emotional children."

Reflect on this now. Where have you been avoiding your own growth? If you reflect on your life as it is today, what would you say is the top action step you have been avoiding taking that you *know* would not only enhance but potentially transform your life if you gathered your courage to get it done? The one you know is causing you stress and wearing you down with every passing minute that it is left unattended to?

Is it mastering the marketing for your business? Is it organising your finances and putting a plan in place? Is it finding your confidence to start dating again? Perhaps it is addressing that health problem, going to the dentist, speaking your truth to that person, clearing your emotional baggage from childhood, booking that plane ticket, letting go of that friend, hiring the team member you need: whatever it is that you know in your bones is required for you to *bloom*.

Ask yourself which unresolved issue is wreaking havoc in your life. Identify which unattended-to task is draining your personal energy. What obstacle do you keep running into because you haven't figured out how to overcome it yet? Perhaps you have made the problem harder than it is. What are you shying away from – or flat out running from – that is keeping your life smaller than you want it to be? Stating what feels like your Achilles Heel right now is the first step to getting beyond it.

It is important to remember that while it is in our animalistic nature to bolt from pain, to run from the beast that terrifies us, it is also in our transcendent spiritual nature to *conquer* what lies before us. It is to not allow our situation to dictate how we feel nor allow the trials and tribulations we meet along the journey to crush our dreams. It is to see *beyond* what bothers us in the here-and-now to a brighter future, the one worth fighting for.

Because we don't want where we have come from to write the rest of our story. Because we know that it is when we are in the ring doing the thing that we unleash our potential. Because we want more for our future and because that fire of determination burns brightly at our core. Because we don't want to live forever as a smaller, fearful, timid version of ourselves – but instead know ourselves as the legend of our own life.

Accept and appreciate the bittersweet nature of life: that you *will* be challenged, guaranteed. That you *will* be required to show up and step up when it counts. That you *will* experience sadness, happiness, comfort, and adversity in equal measures. That you *will* experience doubts and setbacks and failures on the way to the top. That you *will* face your demons, be pushed to your edge, and feel compelled to answer the deepest questions there are.

A life without growth isn't an option – and deep down, you know you wouldn't want it any other way. You don't want a life where you wallow in the shallows or sit on the sidelines watching people play the game. I know in my heart that you want to evolve. You want to feel the blood coursing through your veins, the exhilaration, and the heart-opening satisfaction of knowing that you *did* this; that you leaned into this gift of life and made it yours. That you lived true to yourself. That you lived fully. That you made the most of every moment of your human experience. You want to be ALIVE. It's what you are here for.

At your deepest core, you know that your current circumstances aren't who you are. They are just *where* you are, and in your heart of hearts, you know that the treasure you seek does exist inside the cave you fear to enter, as Rumi wrote so beautifully. You want that treasure. You want the better result, the empowered life, the brighter future, the destiny that is yours and waiting to be claimed.

Who you *become* in the process is worth every ounce of the effort required to tackle that dragon. You *will* be stronger, calmer, more powerful, poised, confident, and badass when you step through the fire and out the other side.

When you confront your fears, when you do the thing you know you need to do, you will realise that you are exponentially more resilient and capable than you originally thought. You will realise that dealing with that problem was liberating and nowhere near as scary as you initially thought. Your self-respect will grow, because tackling the problems that weigh on your mind is the perfect act of self-love.

So, get to it. Meet that task, that opportunity, that obstacle, that challenge, that perplexing riddle, that seemingly insurmountable problem. Roll with the punches. Flow with the current. Twist with the turns. Invest in yourself and focus on your growth. Read the books and learn the skills.

Rise up from the flames and begin again. Draw on your extraordinary human spirit and discover what you are made of. Greet the challenge like a worthy opponent… and then show it who is boss, because the 'you' that is on the other side of the pain you've been dodging is waiting. That is how dreams are made.

32
MONEY REPRESSION

"Don't let money run your life.
Let money help you run your life better."

JOHN RAMPTON

Pretending that you don't want money. Saying that it is "okay" to not have what you dream. Being adamant that money does not and can never buy "happiness" – however you define it. Living on less than you need. Wearing your poverty like a badge of honour. Delaying the importance of setting yourself up financially. All of these resemble the starving artist mentality, where we deny not only the desire but the importance of financial flow and wealth in our life.

Your money repression may very well be undermining your dreams. How? Because it limits your ability to make both a difference and a fortune doing what you love while fulfilling the higher purpose and deeper meaning of your life. How can you maximise your potential, be creative, and unleash your genius, if you spend your entire life in a state of financial survival and stress?

What I know in my heart is that you don't want your debts to drown your dreams or your bills to be bigger than your ambitions for life. You don't want to work for decades barely scraping by without thriving. You also don't want to hold yourself back from the heights of your career because you are too altruistic to admit that you want financial wealth to be a part of your life. You want to form a healthy, intimate, life-long, and meaningful partnership with money. You want more for yourself financially – and it's time for a change.

It's impossible to embrace and create wealth without simultaneously releasing your strong-held and unhelpful judgements about money. The two simply can't and won't go hand-in-hand. For example, if you publicly preach that wealthy people are greedy, but you privately yearn for more. If you believe that the government is evil, the system is corrupt, and taxes are bad, but yet you would love to increase your income ten-fold.

If you think that materialism is greedy, but you truthfully want that nicer house, a car that doesn't break down every second week, and the holiday to the Bahamas in that five-star hotel. This dissonance between your judgements on money and your heartfelt desire for more creates conflict within you and interferes with your birthright to be rich.

Your money judgements will either help or hinder your progress. They will either skyrocket or limit your abundance. They will either be your greatest supporter or play out a full-on game of tug-of-war inside your psyche, undermining your prosperity and blocking you from the opportunities, ideas, and strategies that would enable money to pour into your life. So, be conscious of the conversation about money that happens between your ears. It might sound like this:

Other people are destined to be wealthy, but not me. If I become rich, my family or friends will judge me. I don't want to be seen as snobby. My parents worked hard to raise me and I don't want to disrespect them by out-earning them. Other people work 40 hours a week earning way less than me and I feel bad about that. My God, that person is making a killing. People who own Porsches are wankers. Why don't the wealthy rescue the poor? Tax the rich! No human being needs that much money.

These and every other version of these limiting perspectives, feelings, and beliefs around wealth cause money repression in your life, and money repression breeds money chaos. The simple truth is that money is an unavoidable and powerful part of life – it is a means of exchange, a tool for creating value, a way to enable experiences, a resource to invest in what we believe in. The harder you try to run from your finances and the deeper you try to bury your desire to be provided for amply, the higher your stress levels surrounding money will be.

If you have repressed your need for wealth, it's unlikely that you will set goals for your financial area of life, let alone achieve them. It's unlikely that you will keep your finger on the pulse of your money, let alone set up effective cash-flow management strategies to create solidity and reduce volatility. You will avoid the pivotal details, never plan ahead, ignore your profit margins, and delay the education you need. You will spend your life cash-poor, constantly struggling and falling short of the income you need and stretched to the point of panic.

You won't take care of your money so that it takes care of you nor will you address the essential 'need' for investing in your nest-egg. Instead of being a strategy to support your dreams, money will become the reason you never fulfil them. Your denial and repression of your current situation and future aspirations will only worsen the situation and delay the wealth you deserve. Feelings of lack, envy, righteousness, or the habit of criticising or blaming the rich or blaming money for your misery won't help you to transform your financial destiny.

If you feel guilty or ashamed about wanting, working for, and receiving money, it may help to remember that building wealth isn't just about what you can personally acquire or buy. It's about service. It's about what you can do for the world around you with what is within you. It is about the value you can share, the lives you can touch, and who you can help on your journey… and *that* is not selfish. It is noble. It is courageous and equally selfless. You have immense power to serve people, and you deserve to be rewarded for your service. Embrace the truth of that.

Instead of worrying what other people will think about you as you become richer, focus on the legacy that you can leave. Instead of holding back and suppressing your desire for wealth out of fear of judgement, dedicate your energy and effort into being an inspiration to others. And instead of avoiding conversations, responsibilities, and education that would help you master money, apply yourself and embrace your finances. Do it for yourself, do it for the people you love, and do it for humanity.

Imagine what you could do for the world around you if you became rich financially. Imagine the projects you could fund, the causes you could champion, and the dreams you could bring to life if you stepped in, without hesitation, to your wealth-building journey. IMAGINE the awe-inspiring work you could produce if you were no longer worried about your own survival. Don't you want that for yourself?

It's time to drop the weirdness about money. Lean in. Embrace it. Get curious. Get inspired. Start dreaming. Establish your plan. Manage it well. Enjoy the process. Conquer your financial destiny for yourself and for those you love, for the life you yearn to live, and for the difference you yearn to make. Leave a legacy. Do it with love: create, initiate, and receive wealth so that money never becomes an obstacle to your goals but rather a pathway for your dreams.

33
Money Obsession

"Not everything that counts can be counted and not everything that can be counted, counts."

WILLIAM BRUCE CAMERON

Now it is time to address the other extreme: where becoming *too* focused on money costs us a meaningful life. This is where we become obsessed with our financial status and our monetary gain to the point where it is now the only thing that seems to matter to us. Life, relationships, work – it becomes all about the money and the status of our bank accounts.

How much does that cost? What will I get paid for doing that? When can I get a pay rise? How little can I work for the maximum profit? If I just sell this X, I'll then be able to X for myself and get rich! How much can I make from that? Why is it so hard for me to make easy money? It's a subtle undercurrent that can disconnect you from the flow of ideas, service, and strategies that attract meaningful and sustainable wealth into your life.

Ironically, becoming too focused on the money often blocks it from showing up in our lives and bank balances. Why? Because we get attached to get-rich-quick schemes and don't put in the work required to see it take off. We can worry about money so often that it appears to be the only thing that matters. We allow the size of our bank balance to colour the way that we live. When our financial situation – be that lack or gain – is the dominant thing on our mind, we live from a space of scarcity and greed rather than service and grace.

I have witnessed this at work in my own business. During times in the past when I was concerned about cash-flow and obsessing over my bottom line, I repelled fresh marketing ideas or word-of-mouth referrals, which were the source of my clients and income at the time. It seemed like a magic trick how quickly I could make clients disappear from my life when I worried *too* much about my top-line revenue.

On the flip side, it was miraculous how rapidly I attracted new customers when I focused my attention back on the results that I wanted to help people achieve. When I remembered why I started in my career and how much I love my clients, I became magnetic to wealth opportunities. This became both proof and a valuable lesson that financial flow and prosperity requires us to focus on what we can give just as much as what we can get.

Most people assume that if they just had 'more' money, their problems would be solved and *then* they would have a great relationship with their finances, that *then* they would love and appreciate and enjoy interacting with money. But it doesn't work that way. In fact, it is the other way around. Mindset first, manifestation second. Inner alignment first, outer abundance second. Habits first, results second.

When we are consumed by fear, scarcity, and stress around money – like many people are – it feels near impossible to change our situation. It seems like there will never be enough cash-flow for us to get on top of our bills let alone experience life the way we dream. But it is in these moments where we must change our relationship with money so that we work in harmony with it and, yes, master it, but are never a slave to it. Where we work with it and use it to aid our inspiring and meaningful outcomes but where we do not allow it to define who we are or how much we are worth.

Constantly striving to get ahead financially at any cost can consume you. Just like when we repress our desire for money, we live our life through the lens of price tags and bank balances, and it can cause just as much stress as barely getting by: the stress of never having enough.

There will always be someone who earns more than you, who owns a bigger business, who has a better house, a more expensive wardrobe, a nicer whatever – who is financially richer or more cashed-up than you. That is why it is important to know your 'enough': how much you truly want and need to fulfil your goals and dreams.

Otherwise, you will never be able to pick your priorities, make progress, or know when you have reached your targets. Aimlessly chasing 'more' will cause you to never experience the financial freedom and empowerment you desire and deserve.

Ideals around money have been deeply ingrained into us as part of society: that we are not successful unless we are making a fortune; that we must keep making more and more every year; that we can measure our success and fulfilment in life by the money we make. Although there is some truth to this, it is far from the whole truth. Who we are, what we do, the influence we have on others, what we are known for, and how we feel day-to-day are just as significant, and in some cases, far more than how wealthy we are.

Here's a profound reminder of all the things money cannot buy: your reputation, your deepest relationships, your health, your wisdom, your character, your mental health, your connection with your purpose, your longevity, your authentic friendships, your restful sleep, your career achievement, your body transformation, your respect. The list goes on.

Does money aid these? Yes. But the real work required to create and master any of these lies way beyond the power that money has. They require the core of you: your heart, your mind, your essence, your spirit, your character. They require grit. Determination. Persistence. Time. All that which is immaterial and cannot be bought over the counter. They don't always come easily, but they are worth their weight in gold.

Set yourself up financially. Do well in your business. Maximise your profit margins. Charge properly for your time and your skills. Package your gifts so you can help thousands of people with your uniqueness and your strengths. I'm all for that. But also remember that if life becomes *all* about the money, it loses its true meaning.

It is not about how much you earn. It is the management of it, the appreciation of it, the appreciation of yourself, the vision for your wealth, the structures you implement, and the habits you have that make the difference. It is the daily relationship with it and your approach towards it that defines, unlocks, limits, and shapes your financial reality. It is your heartfelt vision for your financial fortunes combined with your desire to serve people that sets you up for the future you love.

So, let the money you earn be either a means to or a byproduct of your goals in life, not the only goal itself. Give it a deep cause, meaning, and purpose in your life that is not about the money but rather beyond the money.

Appreciate what you have already achieved. Be thankful for the cash in your bank accounts today. Acknowledge yourself for your efforts. Enjoy the view as well as the climb… and be sure to manage your money (and your relationship with it) well so that it never interferes with what you were born to do.

34
CLUTTER AND CHAOS

"Getting organised is a sign of self-respect."
GABRIELLE BERNSTEIN

Although some may believe that being messy is an essential part of the creative process and that life is simply too short to 'tidy up', if your entire life is filled with mess, it can undermine your potential and therefore your dreams.

Imagine trying to build a global business when you can't find your own keys. Or trying to come up with ground-breaking or life-changing ideas when your desk is overloaded with loose bits of paper, and you can't find where you wrote those epic ideas down. Imagine trying to rest deeply at night when there is a mountain of clothes piled up on the floor. Or attempting to complete your master's degree, make a quantum leap in your career, stay on track with your goals, or get ahead in life when your environment is a pigsty.

While bringing order to your life isn't particularly complicated or spiritually deep, the impact that it will have on your state of mind and your ability to perform at your best is profound. This may appear to be OCD, but it works as it is incredibly difficult to find your way forwards if the spaces you live and work in are a disordered mess.

Chaos outside breeds chaos on the inside. Clutter outside equals clutter inside. Clarity outside equals clarity inside. Organisation externally creates organisation internally. Too much 'stuff' cramps your style and clouds your mind. Yet when you can find things easily in the world around you, I am certain that it will help you find things far more easily in the world *within* you which includes your soul's purpose, your goals for the future, your career direction, and the existential answers you seek.

In my opinion, detoxing your life by decluttering is one of the fastest and most effective life hacks to feel clear, calm, and ready to move forwards. A clean and ordered home, office, car, and tech space supports presence of mind, and presence of mind supports feelings of gratitude and joy, our inspiration, creativity, ideas, and solutions. Essentially, when we see clearly around us, we see clearly within us.

Recall a moment when you were travelling. Do you remember how relaxing your hotel room felt? Why was that? Because the room was (hopefully) clear and clean and because (and this is profound) you only took with you what you wanted and needed. Do you recall how free and inspired and light you feel when you walk in nature? How open your mind is and how alive your body becomes when you look at the trees, the sea, the sky?

This is because there is not a shred of human 'stuff' nor material possessions to distract you from the magic of the moment. These are examples of how simplicity in our immediate environment has a deep, soothing, and uplifting effect on our mind and body. It supports us to think clearly, to work without distraction, and to tap into creative flow. This is why we need this type of clarity in the physical spaces where we spend time in order to feel free in our lives.

Here are the most important areas to examine, cleanse, declutter, and organise, to create simplicity and clarity for yourself. Let's start with your foundation: your home. How does your home feel when you walk in the door? Are you holding onto broken, unwanted, uninspiring, or unnecessary items? When was the last time you spring-cleaned your wardrobe? Is it time to unleash your inner Marie Kondo and clear out what no longer sparks your joy?

When was the last time you used *that* item or appliance? Does the thought of opening your cupboards bring you a sense of dread? What does your garage look like right now? Perhaps it is time to overhaul and organise your home space and create a feeling of Zen in every room. It is both the foundation and the springboard for your progress, results, momentum, and dreams. As my half-sister Tanya used to say to me when I was a teenager, "Tidy house, tidy mind."

Next, it is time to simplify your work life. Yes, that means opening, deleting, and sorting out those thousands of unread emails that clog up your inbox. Unsubscribe from those lists you are no longer interested in and categorise your messages. Then, sort out your photos. Archive or delete files that you no longer need. Sort out your paperwork. Upgrade your technology. Create a new folder and file sorting system.

How is your financial life? Is your paperwork filed? Are your bank accounts organised? Are your taxes up to date? Have you organised budgets and set up money management and wealth-building strategies? Financial organisation matters as when you get serious about your money, you show yourself and the universe that you are ready for serious money. It is for this reason that clearing your money clutter could be life-changing.

The same principle applies to the rest of your life: bringing order to your immediate environments sends the message to your inner self and the ether that one, you care about your life and two, that you want to master it. Even knowing where your keys and wallet are at all times contributes to this. The simple things matter.

You already know which area of your life is 'messy' right now. Maybe it is your physical belongings or your clothing or in your digital world or within an enormous pile of unfiled paperwork. Regardless of where your chaos is right now, harness your organising energy and let's get to it.

It doesn't matter if you spend 30 minutes a day or a 30-day time block bringing order to the chaos; it just matters that you do it for yourself and the extraordinary life you deserve. And by the way, as you methodically clean, declutter, and clean, you will find things you forgot you had; long-lost treasures and possessions that move you. In fact, spring-cleaning your life could be one of the most rewarding things you do this year.

Simplicity in all areas creates wellness on all levels. Order produces clarity and clarity produces action, productivity, and mastery. Your mind and body need space to breathe. We must create physical space for your soul to permeate your mind, for your heart to come online, for you to become crystal clear on your direction, and to unleash the tidal wave of magic that wants to flow forth from deep within you.

Yes, it is time to detox what you no longer require, so you can breathe again. It's time to stop tripping over things that you don't need; to release the items and files and folders and 'stuff' that have become unwelcome baggage in your life. To strip out the old so that you can welcome in the new, the fresh, and the inspiring. Give that gift to yourself and experience the freedom of space so your spirit can soar.

35
APPROVAL ATTACHMENT

"A truly strong person does not need the approval of others any more than a lion needs the approval of a sheep."

VERNON HOWARD

The emotional addiction to approval is intense. It lives in our subconscious mind, affecting our daily actions, motivations, efforts, and even the direction of our life. How does it show up? A few things that come to mind are secretly hoping for recognition, doing things with the motive to receive praise, worrying about fitting in, wanting to be liked, or changing your behaviour to get a gold star sticker on your homework.

It is important to recognise that beneath our desire for approval is a beautiful and incredibly powerful desire to be loved for who we are. In moments when we receive approval from others, we tend to feel wanted, valued, respected, and appreciated. We equate these moments to being loved. But in moments where we are rejected or criticised — which most would consider to be the opposite of receiving approval — and especially from our heroes, parents, loved ones, or mentors, we tend to feel small, worthless, or insignificant.

For most, the pain of feeling berated or outcast that drives the desire to be approved of, and therefore loved, typically stems from childhood. There are generally two different dynamics that played out in our upbringing that lead to an attachment to praise and approval as adults.

The first is where no matter how hard we tried or what we did, we couldn't seem to obtain approval from our parents or carers. We strived and tried different strategies and yet our efforts seemed fruitless because maybe we didn't receive the praise that we hoped we would. "Mum, Mum, Dad, Dad, look, look! I did it myself!" The ripple effect of this is that we can enter adulthood with a deep void inside us, yearning for the approval we perceive we didn't receive growing up.

The second is where you received frequent praise, confirmation, and acknowledgement from your parents when you were young. This is where they applauded your genius, recognised your talent, thought you were the most beautiful thing ever, and shone the light on you, celebrating your wins and abilities. You might wonder what is so-called 'wrong' with this because so many people yearn for it. But it can have a shadow side where you become fixated on receiving a parental stamp of approval and now experience low confidence and emotional instability when it appears to be absent.

As an adult, you now believe that in order to be worthy or loved, you MUST succeed, do bigger and better, strive harder, be the best, and be acknowledged for it… or else you are worthless. Simply put, it can feel that your value is based on your accomplishments alone and therefore, the more success you achieve, the more valuable you are. Your outward results become a subtle but intense measure of your worth as a human being.

This can cause the pattern of working to the point of burnout and doing things because you feel starved for recognition – because who would you be without it? Your identity forms perhaps a little too tightly around whether others like you or what you do, rather than whether *you* like you or what you do.

Which of the two resonates for you? Did you not receive approval as a child and so you have been seeking it as an adult? Or were you recognised so frequently for your achievements (or your looks) that now it is hard to live without it? For me, it was the latter. I popped into adult life with an A-Grade student mentality where I expected myself to do well without ever failing or falling short in anything. It was unrealistic, to say the least.

While there is no doubt that this drove me to work hard and find out what I was made of (and I am grateful for that), it wasn't always a recipe for fulfilment – because what I was doing for the world sometimes became more important than what I wanted and needed to do for myself. I often felt that I had to go big or go home and out-do myself regularly. It was only in my late 20s and early 30s that I shed the pressure of consistently performing at a high level – and what a relief that was.

These two different dynamics can be just as extreme as the other. If left unresolved, they can affect the course of our life, both personally and professionally. Our desire to be praised and approved of can influence how hard we work, our priorities, whose opinion we listen to, the mentors we pick, the money we make, the partners we choose, the lifestyle we have, even the way we dress.

Instead of looking to ourselves and asking what *we* think about our work, how *we* feel about our own life, we subconsciously turn to our parents or those who remind us of our parents: our teachers, mentors, employers, and friends. We attempt to achieve the stamp of approval instead of *trusting* ourselves; that we will know what to do next, that our decision is the right one for us, and that we will figure it out even if we stumble along the way.

And instead of feeling and celebrating all of the magic, the sheer power, love, beauty, and humility of our own successes, we rest our fulfilment on whether we are approved of: whether we did enough, did it 'right', or did a 'good job'. What we might not realise is that in doing this, we *shrink* ourselves, become a child again, and look up to a parental figure hoping to hear, "You did good, kid." Instead of being the emotionally mature self that powerfully acts upon and conquers their life and mission in the world, we look for recognition and confirmation on the outside.

It is deep, yes. And it forms some of the most important work for us to do within ourselves: healing the childhood wounding around approval so we can shift our adult patterns. So that we can set ourselves free from the endless search for our acknowledgement and do what is right for us. To fully occupy our own unique place in the world, to walk our original path, to carve out our authentic life on this planet, regardless of whether our parents understand, like, or care much for our choices.

The first step to healing this constant need for acceptance is to recognise it. Start to observe and then catch yourself whenever you do something with an underlying motivation to be liked, wanted, accepted, or approved of. Be honest with yourself about what drives your behaviour and your efforts. Observe your emotions when you are celebrated or praised, or when you are rejected or challenged. Those will tell all.

Are you trying to belong at a great cost? Are you sacrificing what is important to you for a parent? Are you constantly worried about whether your mentors will approve of your success? Worrying whether you are doing your parents or early-life guardians proud? Living your life under the wings or in the shadows of others? Obsessed with how many likes you receive on a social media post? Terrified about receiving fear and criticism?

My wisdom on this is simple: do it because you *love* it, not to be liked. Recognise and approve of yourself more, so you don't yearn for it from others. SEE yourself for who you are. Love yourself. Celebrate your own wins. Build that bank account inside yourself: your confidence and self-respect. Get to work deciding what *you* will do with this life. Get beyond the need for approval so you can discover a drive far more powerful: the calling from your heart and soul.

36
POOR HEALTH

"He who has health has hope and he who has hope has everything."

ARABIAN PROVERB

Your body is your only point of contact with planet Earth. Love it or despise it, nurture it or neglect it, your body is your home here for this short time. It is your vehicle, your temple, your vessel and if it can't support you to do what you ultimately dream of in the world, that would be a great, great tragedy – as you were made incarnate for a reason far more extraordinary than to simply survive.

When our health deteriorates, our body becomes lethargic. Our mind becomes clouded. Our emotions accumulate and intensify. Our energy becomes blocked. Our creativity diminishes. Our sleep becomes unfulfilling. Our mental state withers. Apathy, depression, and fear become the norm. Our lack of wellness restricts our life force energy which in turn, restricts our ability to transform and actualise our life. If your body is sick, how can your spirit soar?

A congested body becomes a congested life. A heavy body becomes a heavy life. A stiff, sore and weak body becomes a sore and weak life. Sluggish digestion equals a sluggish life. It's tough – and yes, sometimes even tougher to heal, to claim and create and maintain the wellness we need to live our best. But what will our path look like if we don't make the commitment to supercharge our wellness?

The following are various ways in which we ignore or repress our body's cries for nurture and nourishment – and along with this, limit our bandwidth to live the life we dream. Food addictions caused by a lack of spiritual fulfilment. A sedentary lifestyle caused by a lack of desire to get up, get out, and LIVE. Taking our body for granted. Stress, the silent killer. Forming habits around unhealthy vices: from overeating crisps, sugar, and high-starch, low-nutrition foods to consuming excess amounts of wine and coffee, to bingeing shows on Netflix to smoking to recreational drugs… fill in the blank. These are all things to watch out for.

When we are seeking to heal our body and reclaim our wellness, I believe in addressing the body over mind connection as much as the mind over body connection. What does this mean? It means recognising that your current state of physical health impacts your mood, your energy levels, and your capacity to thrive. Therefore, you can change your state of mind and therefore your life through the way that you take care of your body. By eating well. By exercising. By taking the right supplements. By balancing your hormones. By changing your morning routine. You can literally unlock higher states of mind and your potential by healing your physical self.

I am certainly not a trained doctor or medical practitioner, but if you want my advice for wellness, try these basic guidelines: clean up your eating, do the emotional healing work, move your body daily, unwind properly, sleep deeply, drink plenty of water, simplify your work life, supplement your nutrition, and detox your system regularly.

The main point I am intending to communicate here is that, yes, our life (emotions, stress, and situations) impacts our health, but our health also impacts our life. In fact, sometimes the fastest way to change your life is to improve your health. When you detox your body, reduce inflammation, eat well, and restore balance in your system, it *will* change you: you will feel like a new person. Therefore, your body is the first foundation to address if you feel stuck, flat, and uninspired right now.

My own profound healing occurred through the discovery of Ayurvedic medicine. In my late 20s, I had extremely high stress levels, leaky gut, low energy, fluid retention, and imbalanced hormones – and I knew something had to change if I was going to fulfil my vision. I committed to my healing journey because I knew that the alternative – allowing it to become worse by delaying my health intervention – would be far more painful. My dedication was worth every sacrifice: I improved my gut health, rebalanced my hormones, lost weight, and best of all, more than doubled my creative and mental energy.

The need to dial up the attention we devote to our health compounds as we age. When we are young, we rarely give thought to the long-term impacts of our daily habits. We are carefree and a little careless (remember those partying days?). Then we reach our thirties and things tend to change. Aches, pains, and ailments often begin appearing and suddenly our health becomes a far higher priority – especially if we have places to go, things to do, and people to see. The importance of combating the effects of time, toxins, lifestyle choices, and stress compounds and hopefully, before it's too late, we make the change to set ourselves up for lasting wellness.

Regardless of which path of healing you find and follow – whether it is through Ayurveda or Chinese Medicine, nutrition courses or naturopathy, or simply listening to and trusting your own physiology – one truth remains: whether you pursue your dreams or not, whether you live boldly or live timidly, whether you rise to the top or give up and hide, you still need your body. It is your partner for whatever kind of life you decide to live.

Your body is the Ferrari for the racetrack of your life. You need it for every single thing that you want to do, feel, see, achieve. So, do your best not to allow your indulgences to override the desire to live a meaningful life full of energy, movement, deep rest, and adventure. Address anything and everything that damages your wellness and interferes with the natural flow of your physical life force energy. If that means overhauling your diet or your work rhythms or your social circles or educating yourself so you can know better and do better, it is worth it – because YOU are worth it.

Find the discipline and drive required to make the changes because they will not only prolong but enhance every single day of your life. Make regular sleep schedules, walking, nutritious foods, massage, magnesium baths, stretching, natural therapies, ambient light, deep breathing, and healing your new normal. Create a performance plan get on with what you are here for. Heal your body so that you can fulfil your purpose.

37
IGNORING INNER GUIDANCE

*"Have the courage to follow your heart and intuition.
They know what you truly want to become."*

STEVE JOBS

Ignoring the guidance that we feel and hear within us is a surefire way to not only undercut our potential to do great things, but also make a mess of our life. Just to be clear, I am not talking about the inner voice (or voices) that sound like this: *Why is he such a butthead? Why doesn't everything go my way? No matter what I do, I can't get ahead. This pizza sucks. I hate this. What is that person wearing? What should I wear tomorrow? I feel so lost. The rain annoys me. Why can't I figure out my purpose?*

I am referring to the inner voice that comes from a higher and deeper place within you, far beyond your very human (and somewhat entertaining) train of thought. It is the voice that speaks from the deeply spiritual space inside you that is greater than your circumstances, the state of your body, how much money you make, who you are dating, or how many online followers you have right now. It is the voice of your higher self. Your soul. Your infinite, ethereal self. It is the voice that is connected, illuminated, wise, and inspired – and it is an ultimate source of guidance that is within you, 24 hours a day.

Even after acknowledging and listening to my own inner guidance for my entire adult life, I still find myself feeling amazed at how *right*, how specific, and how precise my higher voice of reason and inspiration is. How does 'she' know? How can my divine self *know* so intimately what is right for me? How does she know what I need and when I need it, and exactly when to speak to me? How can my soul's guidance be so, so accurate about what is and is not right for me? How can my inner voice be so damn smart, so inspiring, so insightful, so wise?

I barely have words for how profound and life-altering it has been to follow the knowing within me over the years – and I have lost count of how many moments in which my inner voice has spoken and guided my path. Now, I am so certain about and so convinced of her power and significance that when 'she' speaks, I stop what I am doing so that I can listen carefully with a deep sense of wonder and intrigue about what she wants to say. I want to *know* what message she has for me, what step she wants me to take next, and what guidance she wants me to receive.

I feel humbled by the sheer number of times where my inner self has bailed me out of what would have been a dodgy situation (including intimate relationships, by the way) or guided me towards an opportunity. From telling me to take a jacket with me because it was cold outside (yep!) to letting me know when it was time to end a relationship to what to offer my customer next, she has filled my life with protection, with creativity, and with love. But that is what our inner voice does: it guides us to the life that is POSSIBLE. The one we deserve. It wants us to flourish.

If we ignore our inner guidance, chaos ensues. We wonder why that person is taking advantage of us, but we didn't follow our intuition when it said to walk away earlier. We muse over why we are having so much trouble with our client even though our first instinct was that they would be difficult to deal with. We question why our intimate partnership is so unfulfilling when our inner voice told us to leave months ago. So many of our human struggles are caused by our denial of that which we know from within.

Following your inner guidance is not just a whacky spiritual concept. It is a strategy for success. It can change or even save your life as it steers you towards what is for you and away from that which isn't. Your inner guidance will nudge you when it is time to move forward, to take action, to slow down, to speed up, or to go in a different direction entirely. If you pay attention to and work *with* it, it will steer you towards the meaningful career path, the business model that suits you, the opportunities designed for you, and the relationships that enhance your life.

What is even more extraordinary is that your inner guidance is online and available 24 hours a day, ready and willing to assist you in your human journey of reaching for the stars; of overcoming your hardships; of fulfilling your destiny. You have an inner financial advisor, an inner personal trainer, a health coach, a relationship consultant, and a business mentor inside your own mind. And so, while you will no doubt turn to few or many mentors along your path, you do generally know what to do to master your life: which powerful action to take, what needs sorting out next, where to go and when, and who to connect with.

If you become quiet for a moment and ask yourself, "What is my next step?" or "What would be the best use of my time and energy today?" – the answer will be there. It might take a minute or an hour for your inner self to respond, but it will respond. The answer will come to you. Have faith in that and be patient, because developing a strong relationship with your inner guidance will invite more wisdom into your life – and it *will* be the coach, the mentor, and the oracle you need for your holistic success in this world.

It's not woo-woo or psychic or psychotic (ha-ha) to listen and respond to that voice within you. On the contrary, it is how you stay sane and navigate your way to a brighter future. It is how you know what to do next, how you find your direction, how you make vital decisions, how you find your way through the impossible and do the extraordinary.

I truly believe that the universe at large has bigger, bolder, brighter plans in mind for you than you do for yourself and your life today – and your inner voice is an expression of that. It is your personal on-demand connection to the all-knowing and all-seeing intelligence that loves and wants the best for you.

It is the light shining a pathway through the darkness, the voice of reason, hope, and healing when you feel lost, and the most powerful guide you will ever have. Even as you read this right now, your higher guidance is trying to take you to where you want to be. So, connect with the quiet space within you. What is your inner voice saying to you?

38
Shyness

"All our dreams can come true if we have the courage to pursue them."
Walt Disney

Have you ever watched someone who is right out there in the world, living boldly, and doing their thing whilst wishing you could do the same? Or do you look at your heroes, your mentors, your gurus, or your teachers, and wonder where their relentless courage comes from?

Perhaps you generally feel so shy that putting yourself out there for the world to see is a terrifying thought… but on a spiritual level, you feel *ready* to blast through those nerves and into the stratosphere. There are two things that you can address to help you achieve this: one, a fear of being seen, and two, being so timid that you keep your dream at an arm's length.

Let's start with the fear of being seen, as this is both a pressing and relatable fear for many people. In fact, it is often the number one reason my clients tell me they hold back from their mission, and we all know that public speaking is the number one fear for most people because of the visibility it gives us. The idea of having thousands of eyes watching us can trigger a full-body panic response and cause us to cower in the shadows instead of basking in the light.

While the fear of being seen is undoubtedly connected to a fear of being misunderstood or rejected, it typically stems from a fear of the world seeing something that we don't love about ourselves. Although you may feel afraid of people seeing your whole self, the truth is typically that there is a part of you, or a part of your life, that you feel ashamed of and therefore are uncomfortable with people knowing about.

For example, you don't want to become famous because the world might find out that you used to have a drug addiction or that you failed in your first business or that you have peculiar sexual interests – it happens. We all have these things. Or you are afraid that if you become a public figure known by thousands of people, the world will discover you are not *that* nice, funny, or smart, and so you hide out for fear that you will be exposed, judged, or called a hypocrite.

The simple antidote to the fear of being seen is to work on loving, without condition, all parts of yourself, your life, and your story. This means opening your heart to all that you are, all that you have been, and all that you have done and healing the shame that causes you to run from the light.

When we feel ashamed of a part of ourselves or something that happened in our past, we unconsciously expend precious energy trying to hide those parts of us from the world. It causes us to shrink ourselves, to do less, earn less, and undermine opportunities that light our heart up.

Whether our shame is for past 'failures' or chaotic relationships or sexual experiences or poor financial choices, it is time to heal it. To find the love in it. To remember that any judgement we experience from those around us only mirrors their own shame and pain. To make peace with it all so that even if someone did find out about it (which they may never do) or asked you about it (which is unlikely), you would be fine with it. When you love all parts of you, you don't mind your whole self and the fear of being seen dissolves. Love is the healer.

This next message is for all those who are afraid to rock the boat, who are holding back on their divine mission because they know that it is likely to challenge people. Who feel too timid to ask for what they want and speak up for their needs, let alone set an audacious goal and go after it. Who are sacrificing their desires and dreams, barely daring to voice their vision. Who are too busy being polite to be powerful. Who are keeping their fire, their legacy, and their leadership small.

If this resonates for you, then let me ask this: are you living inside an expectation that you are meant to be 'nice' all the time? Are you too worried about what people will think of you to do what is inside your heart and soul? If so, what will be the long-term cost of this if you keep biting your tongue and delay doing what you feel called to do? What opportunities will you miss? What money will you leave on the table? Are you so concerned about the rules and whether it is acceptable to do what you dream that you are suffocating your potential?

Perhaps you have been holding onto the idea that it is impossible to achieve success without stepping on toes along the way – and I want to let you know that it *is* possible to rise to the top with grace. It *is* possible to speak your truth and fulfil your life's work from a place of poise, and great achievement won't make you 'impure'. Instead, it will magnify all those extraordinary parts of you that gave rise to your success to begin with. It will amplify the very essence and core of your character which, whether or not you have realised it, is a GIFT to the world.

Being outspoken and bold didn't come naturally for me as a child. It took me until my young adult life to find my voice and my courage to use it: to set boundaries, to ask for what I wanted, and to give myself permission to live an outrageously authentic and original life. But with my desire to write, speak, and inspire humanity, came the confidence that enabled me to stand out and shine. To meet the world face-to-face, willing to be and share my full self regardless of the outcome.

The same can happen for you – and it will. You CAN find your confidence, your courage, your worth, your value – and you will. You CAN put yourself out there, way out there, for humanity to know – and it's time to.

Yes, the world might challenge your ideas. People might not understand you. You might be rejected, mess up a speech, or fall flat on your face. Sometimes you will be judged for who you are and questioned about your actions. But that is what will make your life an interesting and worthwhile story and the ultimate journey in personal expansion.

In life, you can run and hide, or you can rise and thrive. It's up to you. Will you cower in the shadows or learn to be bolder? Will you sit on the sidelines or fall in love with stepping up and stepping out? Will you live your life being so careful and controlled that you miss out on all the fun?

Remember, at the end of your years you will look back and assess your time here. You will ask yourself, "Did I make the absolute most of each day?" Make sure the answer is a resounding "Yes" – and don't settle for anything less.

39
CREATIVITY OVERLOAD

"The world needs dreamers, and the world needs doers. But above all, the world needs dreamers who do."

SARAH BAN BREATHNACH

This topic is for the highly creative people of this world. The ones whose minds are filled and flooded with a continuous flow of ideas and visions. Ideas for books, content, businesses, products, solutions, new approaches. Visions of a 'better' world, a new and improved way of living and a brighter future for humanity. I see you, hear you, and feel you – because I am you.

You have a gift for ideas. You see things that other people in this world don't. You have a unique and valuable perspective. You care deeply and dream fearlessly. You are the dreamer that this world needs. The visionary. The one who is more likely to take a risk, launch a company, lead an industry, revolutionise a system, bring about a much-needed upgrade, or produce work that touches and changes lives.

What I also know is that being a visionary like this can come hand-in-hand with what I call 'creativity overload'. Put simply, creativity overload is where you have so *many* ideas that the sheer volume of them leads to overwhelm, confusion, and inaction. With a million thoughts flying left, right, and centre all day every day, it is nearly impossible to find your focus for long enough to act on your ideas and build momentum – and that can be defeating for your income, fulfilment, achievement. Your energy becomes scattered, and your body becomes stressed as you change gears constantly, jumping between five tasks at once, burning yourself out and feeling impatient: *Why can't my idea just happen already?*

To master our extraordinary creativity, we *must* learn to manage the ideas within us so that they can be made manifest in the world around us. We must learn to filter, organise, and prioritise our ideas so they can materialise. If we don't learn to manage our brilliant mind, we will end up dreaming without doing and visualising without manifesting.

Years will pass by, causing us to feel depressed about our lack of tangible real-world progress. But when we find an effective approach to simplify the constant stream of creative thought and bring our creations to life – be it an artwork, a product, a book, a business, a revolutionary brand – just WOW.

Here is a three-step process to help you overcome creativity overload. One, write all your ideas down as they come to you. This will transfer the ideas out of your mind which will create space for even better ideas or for you to think your existing ideas through. Two, keep your ideas organised.

Don't allow yourself to have a zillion thoughts on a zillion pieces of paper strewn throughout your home, car, and office. Keep them in one place. Group your similar ideas together. For example, collate all the notes for your book in one place or all your product ideas for business in the same notebook. Give your ideas a home.

The three most important documents in my life are my journal (where I document my spiritual insights and do emotional breakthrough work), my Dream Life Plan (where I map out how I would love my life to be), and my business plan (where I keep my ideas for my career and company in a cohesive format). These documents help me to organise my endless stream of thoughts, feelings, and ideas into an epic game plan – and I am certain that finding *your* approach will change your life the way it has mine.

Then finally, and this is step three, learn to push your projects *through* time, through the days, weeks, months, and years. In short, this means working on one or two key projects at a time. This will allow you to tap into unparalleled levels of genius as you concentrate your precious energy into one thing in each phase – and the quality of your work will skyrocket.

It is likely that you will still receive new ideas for the longer-term projects as you work on the short-term ones. Simply make a note and file those for later to give you the satisfaction of knowing you have documented it for when it *is* time to work on that idea. Keep your focus on what counts most, first.

Here are some questions to help you decide on your next priorities might be. Which project feels like it comes next? What idea would make the biggest difference when acted upon? What do you have the most energy for at this moment? Which one inspires you most AND could make the biggest impact on your life right now?

Train yourself to feel into *when* to do things. Develop an acute sense for timing and recognise that not everything can be or needs to be worked on today or every day. This will allow you to find a forward-moving flow where you can connect all your ideas together, channel the many brilliant thoughts you have into a single direction and build a phenomenal career in the process. This is the strategy that works for me. Find the one that works for you.

It takes discipline to slow down and sort through your many ideas to decide which ones will serve your higher destiny – your big-picture vision – best and to then set your focus towards them, but it is *necessary* for your greatness. It also requires far more patience than you can probably imagine to allow your ideas to take form properly, to see the idea through to a reality, to think it through until it's a "banger", as my friend Codey Orgill says.

I know that the idea itself is probably far more pleasurable than the reality and journey of actually fulfilling it because of the work involved to do so. But that doesn't mean it isn't worth the effort. In fact, in many cases, the pursuit of the idea turns out to be more meaningful than the moment when it first crossed your mind – because manifesting our concepts into reality is where the full impact is. It is where our ideas touch the planet.

Unexpressed ideas have unfulfilled potential within them that is just waiting to be tapped into. They are power and greatness simply waiting to be expressed. This is why letting your ideas run rampant without also doing something *with* those ideas will cause frustration in your life. This is because your ideas don't pop into your mind to sit on a shelf or be tucked away in a notebook. They come to you to be explored, to be expressed, to be manifested.

Too many highly creative people are more interested in the 'idea high' than getting in the trenches to turn that idea into a reality – but the world doesn't need more ideas. It needs more ideas in motion. It needs YOUR ideas in motion. Your world-changing, life-shifting, innovative, heartfelt, and inspiring creations. Your unique method, your original perspective, your revolutionary research, your teachings, your profound writings, your artworks, your performances, your magic.

You have extraordinary creative abilities and a potent creative energy. But they must be harnessed, otherwise you will spend your whole life playing in the sandpit without ever building a castle. You want to know the satisfaction of your ideas taking flight. So, shift out of creativity overload and into action-taking flow – and touch the world with your presence and projects.

40
Overthinking Things

"If overthinking burned calories, I'd be a supermodel."
Anonymous

All those thoughts. Round and round they go inside your head. One after the other, an endless stream of chatter, a continual flow of information, and an inner dialogue that never seems to quieten down. Are you going a little crazy yet? Although a busy brain can give us the illusion that we are being productive – because our train of thought is focused on important problems and projects all day long – it can be counterproductive when it comes to creating tangible momentum in our lives.

For some, overthinking will end up being the reason that their dreams either don't manifest at all or take far longer than they could have to come true. A thinking session that results in an action and then an outcome is valuable – invaluable, even. But thoughts that just loop over and over, that are tinged with anxiety or scarcity, just cause stress.

How do you know when you are overthinking? Your body starts to feel tense. Your breathing becomes shallow. Your head is noisy all day long and you can't sleep at night. You feel exhausted from being 'on' all the time. You are no closer to solving a problem despite the enormous amount of mental energy you have expended thinking about it. You continue to have the same thoughts over and over. You go around and around instead of upward and forward.

In order to lessen our brain noise, focus our thoughts, and produce results for ourselves, we need to understand what causes overthinking. A friend once suggested that overthinking is a result of holding onto pride. In other words, you don't want to risk the chance of ridicule or failure, so you keep thinking over *how* to do it instead of actually *doing* it. Fair play – and highly relatable. I once sat on a marketing idea for 12 months before actioning it because I was afraid it wouldn't work… which it did, when I stopped thinking about it and launched it.

But overthinking can also be a result of fear. This might be fear of the unknown, fear of failure, or the fear of success, as many may describe it. The overthinking then becomes a safety and survival strategy, to reduce the chances of ever having to face that fear. Or – and here's a deep one to consider – being in your head all the time can be an unconscious tactic to avoid *feeling*. This is where you have so much pent-up emotion inside you that you are terrified to slow down and relax into your body because it might trigger a full-blown meltdown.

Not believing with deep-seated faith and certainty that things *can* and *will* work out for *you* in this life can also cause overthinking. This is where we think, think, think, and even take small actions on our thoughts, but never quite reach where we want to be, because deep down we don't feel that we deserve what we are aiming for. Our overthinking then becomes the symptom of a lack of self-worth that lives under the surface.

It is also possible that, on a physical level, your body is 'vata aggravated' as is referred to in Ayurvedic medicine. Put simply, there is too much air or 'vata' trapped in your system in places where it shouldn't be. This causes your digestive tract to be unsettled, your energy to be chaotic and ungrounded, and your nervous system to be perpetually agitated. This leads to a noisy brain, sleep issues, and an inability to relax and go with the flow.

What causes *you* to overthink? Is it stress? Too many incomplete tasks and open loops? Too many ideas? Fear of failing? Mental and physical exhaustion? Fear of slowing down? Reflect on this carefully for yourself because staying in a pattern of thinking endlessly without acting courageously can push away and undermine precisely the thing that you yearn for. In fact, overthinking typically delays the discovery of our purpose and the clarity we need, as it drowns out the profound voice of our heart and soul amidst the noise of ineffective and unhelpful thinking.

As well as setting clear goals, mastering your time management, and healing your emotions, a powerful antidote to overthinking is to do something completely different that distracts and then quiets and calms your mind. Give your brain a break; a chance to slow down and reset itself. Go out with friends, take a walk, meditate, run, listen to music, lift weights, journal, paint, work in the garden, spend time with your dog. Find *your* way to switch your mind off.

As Cal Newport wrote about in his profound book *Deep Work,* your conscious mind has the ability to solve problems within certain parameters, but your unconscious mind has infinitely more neuronal bandwidth. When we log off or walk away for a moment and seek to actively switch our conscious mind 'off', we allow the thoughts, ideas, and solutions we need to drop into the space we have created inside our mind. In short, we *need* downtime to get clear, to produce results, to unleash our genius, and to know what to do next.

Physical activity is also powerful for combating overthinking as it guides you back into your body while also burning off excess cortisol that can cause overthinking to begin with. When we become grounded into and connected with our bodies, we become present. We can sense, tune in to, and feel the subtle energies within and around us. Our mind relaxes and opens as our body unwinds. Our senses become heightened, and we can see details we missed before. The movement frees us from the chaos of overthinking.

It is not so much the strategy you use to quiet your thoughts that counts; it's that you apply it, that you find an effective way to tap back into your heart, your soul, your body, and the flow of life. When we are continually caught in our thoughts, we not only disconnect from the world around us and waste time and energy, but don't realise that there are many people who can support us with what bothers us and who have solutions to the problems that plague us. This is the gift in getting 'out of our mind'. In the process, we get out of our way.

We allow spontaneous inspiration, deep feeling, our own wisdom, our higher guidance, the love we are surrounded by, and the greater intelligence of the universe and this life to be our source and our support. We stop worrying so much, we relax, and things become far simpler. It is in that space where we flourish; where we allow what is beyond us to guide our life on Earth and help us to fulfil our destiny.

41
UNDERMINING YOUR DREAMS

"What if I fall? Oh, but my darling, what if you fly?"
ERIN HANSON

You have two choices in your life: you can talk yourself into achieving your dreams or you can talk yourself out of fulfilling them. Talking yourself *into* your dreams means looking for the way *through* the wall. It means being determined to beat the odds and pushing forwards boldly, no matter how slim your chances of success might seem. It means never allowing the internal dialogue of 'What if I can't do this?' become the dominant voice of your life. And it means saying "Yes" and giving it a try, knowing that even if you can't see all the steps yet, you will figure it out along the way.

It's showing up for that gig, even when your palms are sweating and you're terrified. It means visualising the results manifesting, the miracle occurring, the opportunity appearing, the door opening, the success happening, the blessings coming. It is being on your side in every situation, no matter how you feel in the heat of the moment, picking yourself up again every time you fall, and being your most reliable coach through the toughest stages of your journey. It is focusing on the silver lining instead of the storm clouds.

Undermining Your Dreams

If you are talking yourself *out* of your dreams, however, then you will be relentlessly focused on all the reasons that you think you can't have what you want. You will be consumed by fear and expect the worst. You will pick your goals apart before you have left the starting block. You will aim small with your success so that you won't be disappointed… or you won't even try to do what you feel born to do.

You will rule your ideas out before exploring their potential. You will block support and stifle the flow of receiving in your life. You will be obsessed with the negative side of the coin. You might even tell the world around you a story of all the reasons you *can't* be, do, or have what you dream. Or you will pretend that what you yearn for doesn't matter to you anywhere near as much as it truly does.

Instead of pursuing what we want with enthusiasm, we talk ourselves out of our dreams, and then we fill our life with a myriad of other things – priorities, commitments, obligations, responsibilities – that *seem* important in an attempt to fill the void where our dreams would otherwise be. It's no way to live, to sacrifice what brings us meaning because we got in our own way. We are often the biggest reason that we don't pursue what lights us up in life – from our personal relationships to the heights of our soulful dreams – because we keep talking ourselves *out* of what we want (writing that made me well up with tears).

If you know that this is true, and if you are hungrier than ever for an entirely new lease on your life, then maybe it is time to change from the inside-out and get on your side for good. To admit your negative-Nancy tendencies decide that it is time for a change. To decide that it is time for a more empowering approach and attitude towards to your own future. To believe in greater possibilities and take a divinely guided chance on your destiny.

Pay attention to those quiet voices inside your mind, the ones that run a subtle commentary on your life, your work, your career, your gifts, your future. The one that reveals how you *truly* feel and what you *really* think about what you are doing, about your goals, and about what you can achieve. That will give you an honest measure on whether you are backing or berating yourself from within.

And from there, you can work on it. You can catch yourself in the act when your doubts pop up. You can intercept your own thought patterns and focus on the outcome not the obstacle. You can write a new story to tell yourself about your life; one where you do what you love and fulfil your wildest dreams. You can push yourself to *believe* in yourself, in your goals, in your aspirations, in your vision.

Do the difficult thing – clarify your purpose, your goals, and your dreams – and then get into motion. And when you greet obstacles, treat them as a stepping stone, not a dead end. Train yourself to look for the way through instead of taking the current outcome as the final outcome. Push yourself to ask for help, to talk to experts, to see beyond what is in front of you. Discipline yourself to rise to a challenge rather than run away from it. In the heat of the moment, tell yourself inside, "I can do this."

Start with the small things, because then when it comes to the bigger things, you will be *ready*. You will be behind yourself, backing yourself like the greatest cheerleader of all time. Even when you stumble, you will find a way to pat yourself on the back and say, "Keep going."

And even on your toughest of days and in moments when you are breaking apart, your inner self will whisper to you, "You've got this."

It might take weeks, months, or years to train yourself to back yourself. But if you don't at least attempt to get on your side more, to work *with* yourself, then you will make your life exponentially harder than it needs to be. The journey to find your purpose will feel impossible, achieving your goals will feel difficult, you will struggle in ways you don't need to, and ultimately, end up living a life filled with regrets.

If you don't believe in yourself, who will? If you don't carry yourself through the tough times, how can anyone support you? And if you don't persist with your calling despite your own insecurities, how can you experience the abundance that is available to you? You can sell yourself whatever kind of life you want. So, what is it going to be? Is it going to be the life of surrendered attempts and small shots? Or will it be a life where *you* are the wind in your own sails? The life where you say, "Screw it" and just go for it?

42

Flying Solo

"Anything is possible when you have the right people to support you."

Mary Copeland

This is a message for all those dreamers who are trying to do it all themselves. Who are taking it all on, with their walls up against the world, and who think they have to do it alone. Those who are pushing themselves too hard and causing unnecessary misery in their lives. Those who are suffering in silence because they are carrying a load too heavy for their own shoulders. Those who are holding on so tightly to doing it all that they are not allowing themselves to prioritise what they love.

It's time to change your approach to life, to work, and to achievement. Why? Because you know that a weighed down and stressed-out version of 'you' isn't the optimum you. To unlock your fullest potential and fly, you must be supported to perform at your best… and you can't make your impact on the world when you are trying to run the entire world.

Are you trying to do it all because you feel that you must? Are you resisting support because you would feel weak if someone stepped in and supported you? Are you blocking help because you are trying to prove to yourself or someone else that you are strong? Are you refusing help because you are afraid someone else might take the credit for your effort? Are you being stubborn or controlling or afraid to let go of the reins in some areas of your personal and professional life?

Are you perhaps a little too righteous, thinking that *only* you can do the job well and so you never let go and let others step in and shine? Do you believe that if you don't do it all yourself, you won't have earned your riches and success? Or do you fly solo because you simply don't feel worthy of the support you so badly need? Where are you restricting support – and what is that about for you?

I understand the desire, the need, the drive to show yourself what you are made of. I also know how satisfying it is to tackle a challenge, to push yourself, to break limits, to empower your life, and to set an example for yourself of what is possible. To know that you changed your life – YOU – and that it was with your very own hands that you turned it all around from the inside out, blood, sweat, tears, and all. To hustle and create and conquer.

But I also know that we truly can go so much further when we travel together than when we try to do it all alone. When we allow others to use their unique strengths alongside our unique strengths. When we team up for a common purpose, a shared mission, a meaningful cause, an inspiring dream. When we meet with one goal in mind and see what we can create. When we have the same end outcome in mind that moves us, and we each use *our* magic to create *the* magic.

I, for one, know that I could not and would not have come this far without the support of those around me. I wouldn't have overcome depression, started my business, spoken on stages, launched global projects, run a company, published my many books nor achieved my heartfelt dreams if I didn't have certain special people in the wings playing a vital role along the way.

In the significant turning points of my journey, they were right by my side, allowing me to lean on them in moments of doubt, weakness, or fear. They each made a crucial contribution to my personal growth, to my work, to my business, and to my life, to help in making it all that it can be. And together with the deep difference I have been blessed to make in the lives of so many, that is where I have experienced some of the deepest love I've ever felt the love of knowing I am not alone and simultaneously completely worthy of being championed towards my dreams. Where would I be without them?

I don't know why you feel that you must fly solo – only you know that. But what I do know is that you deserve to be supported on your journey. You deserve a co-pilot. A person or people who can be the air beneath your wings, lift you up when you are down, steady you when you feel weak. People who can take a chance on you, bet on you, open doors for you, work for you, and conquer the world with you. People who encourage you and who would fight for you, and who can't wait for you to hit it BIG.

Trying to do it all yourself not only weighs you down but slows you down from achieving what you have set out to do. You only have a certain amount of mental-emotional-spiritual bandwidth and it's impossible to master every single skill or do every single task yourself. It's wiser to discover and then double down on your one or two areas of greatest strength; your gifts and the areas where your extraordinary value is.

It's time to let things go. To admit your areas of weakness. Team up with people who love doing what you dislike, who excel where you lack skills, who thrive where you feel drained, who would leap at the chance to be there for or with you on the mission. Let the angels in. That is how you fulfil your dreams; by surrendering a little control; by trusting in your team; by creating the right support systems to carry you through.

Yes, support others, but allow yourself to be supported, too. Remember that you also matter. You are not designed to go it alone, to fight the fight alone, to figure it all out alone, or to be alone in this world. You are part of humanity, and you are surrounded by people who can help, guide, lead, work with, and inspire you. You just need to decide to open up and let them in – to let the love in – so you can SHINE.

43
Chasing Destinations

"Nothing is more precious than being in the present moment. Fully alive and fully aware."

Thich Nhat Hanh

Between my mid-20s and early 30s, my career growth accelerated significantly. I founded my company at the age of 26, launched global projects, and doubled my revenue three years in a row. I was determined to serve the world, following my heartfelt calling and the fire inside me to *do more* with myself, with my gifts, and with my life. I wanted to make an impact fulfilling my purpose.

The underbelly of this extraordinary time of expansion was that the pace of my work life had sped up so much that I sometimes felt like my head was spinning. Many people needed me, from my team to my clients, and I often had a few too many projects on my plate for what I could comfortably handle. This intensity in my business triggered an underlying sense of urgency that started to cause digestive issues and burnout in my body, as I shared earlier in the book.

Because my days were insanely busy, I sometimes felt that I was missing the depth and beauty of my own journey. I wasn't *feeling* with full openness the love and magic in my life the way I did in my young adult life. The other side effect was that I wasn't truly appreciating myself for the difference I was making in the lives of my readers and customers. A new week would begin, I'd blink, and it was Friday again. Suddenly I turned 30, then 32, then 34. My life felt like it was flying by at an alarming rate. I realised I was chasing destinations – and something had to change.

What I know with certainty today is that moving at a frantic pace and perpetually living in the future striving for the next big thing and missing the 'now' isn't the most fulfilling way to go through life. Rushing around feeling wound up, stressed, and desperately trying to get ahead without also being in *this* moment right here only causes us to feel that we have never done nor achieved enough. It can disconnect us from the possibility and the potential that is around us and within us today. It can cost us the healing, the love, and a humbling appreciation of the present moment.

Therefore, it is VITAL that we stop and see how far we have come, that we celebrate our life as it happens, otherwise we will miss out on the exquisite deeper meaning of it all. It is by smelling the roses occasionally and slowing down that we can not only appreciate and love ourselves for the effort we have put in, but also refine our focus for the future.

What worked? What did I enjoy? Did I love doing that? Does this still feel like my path? These moments of quiet reflection on our journey so far allow us to thank ourselves, to thank the people who have encouraged and pushed and supported us, and to thank life for bringing us here to begin with. It fuels us for our future and all that we are yet to achieve. Without it, we are living manic lives that pass by in an instant.

How do we overcome this feeling of running behind and of never being where we want to be because there is always so much work to do? We strike a beautiful, enriching balance between striving and enjoying. Between gratefully accepting what we have while aspiring for more. Between acknowledging our progress and pursuing what is next. We feel our way to our own intuitive balance between working in our lives and on our lives.

It also helps to remember how deeply we need simplicity, time, and space to perform and thrive well. On a mental, emotional, physical, and spiritual level, we need slowness just as much as we need speed in order to create momentum. We *need* room to breathe, unwind, and rejuvenate. To let the dust settle, to regroup, and to move forward with gusto.

These precious and profound moments of stillness on our journey also give us access to what I call the 'cosmic inbox'. The cosmic inbox is the beautiful phenomenon that occurs when you take a step back from your life, interrupt the busyness and just 'be' for a moment, whether that is for an hour, a day, or a week. As you slow down – as you calm your body and quiet your thoughts – you create space inside your mind for new information to 'drop in'.

When your body relaxes and your mind finally becomes still, ideas and insights will start to pop into your mind. You might suddenly find a solution for that problem or come up with a strategy that might work better. Or you will receive intuitive guidance on who to connect with next. You might experience a life-changing breakthrough or receive life-altering insights. This phenomenon that naturally occurs when we become present is extraordinary.

I often imagine that the greater power of the universe and my higher self was simply waiting for my mind to become 'empty' for a moment so it could deliver the information I needed: whether that is a book title, a solution to a client's problem, a personal insight, or a product idea.

The older we get, the more we confront the uncomfortable truth of our mortality and the fact that life is short. It is scary how quickly it creeps up on you. But we can choose not to make it even shorter by rushing our way through it, moving frantically and impatiently through every day, every week, every meal, and every conversation trying to reach some often unknown and sometimes illusive destination.

While we are part of the human race, it doesn't mean we have to race our way through life… or that life is a race at all. Maybe the true beauty of life is in the simplicity, the slowness, the delicious depths of the present moment. Maybe we discover the true meaning of life when we savour the love, the wisdom, and, yes, the potential, within each minute.

You are always there and never there at the same time. You are suspended between your past, whatever it may have been, and your future, whatever that will be, perfectly poised to make the very most of each moment that life has given you. Don't skip over them. Slow down and feel. Think. Reflect. Express. Connect. Become. Allow yourself to unwrap and enjoy each moment. That's where all the magic is.

44
Blaming and Complaining

*"A thankful person is thankful under all circumstances.
A complaining soul complains even in paradise."*

Bahá'u'lláh

Blaming and complaining is one of the fastest ways to make ourselves miserable, lonely, and depressed in life. What I know with certainty is this: bitching at the government, finding fault in every experience we have, judging people and their actions, pointing the finger, and seeing the wrong, the bad, the ugly in the world is a surefire way *not* to get what we want.

Instead of moving through life with graciousness and appreciation, we repel blessings away from us. Our negative attitude deflects possibility and opportunity out of our lives and keeps us stuck where we don't wish to be. Our unrealistic expectations on the universe to bend to and support our reality one hundred percent of the time causes frustration. And our inability to ever be pleased by the people, places, and events we experience makes it impossible for us to find the fulfilment we yearn for. We become trapped inside our own approach to life.

Why would you keep giving gifts to an ungrateful person? Or continue to do favours for someone who never says thank you for your effort? This is the principle and power of our energy and actions at work: that what we send out to the world around us truly does become mirrored back to us in what we attract, experience, and receive from people and life itself. In fact, I can say with ease that living with a generally grateful mentality towards the universe has made every single one of my dreams come true to date. Gratitude comes from humility and the heart, and these are magnetic. They draw miracles towards us.

What is tricky about blaming and complaining is that sometimes we aren't aware that we are doing it. We don't realise that we are focused on looking for what we don't like or finding reasons that someone or something doesn't meet our expectations. And so, we must sneak up on and catch ourselves in the act. We must *notice* when we are ranting beyond the point where it is useful, notice when complaining about a situation is draining our life force, and know when it is time to rein ourselves in.

We can do this by observing the words we speak and the thoughts we have each day. How are we perceiving the world around us? Are we viewing events, people, places, and situations through a lens of negativity? Or are we living and looking at our life with an open mind and heart, seeing *beyond* the surface and discovering the blessing in each experience.

If it is always someone else's fault, you will rob yourself of the power and freedom to create your life your way. And if you keep picking apart each experience, person, or opportunity, you will deny yourself the beauty that is all around you. When we engage in complaining and blaming, so much so that it becomes our mode of operating, we block out solutions. Assistance. Support. Wisdom. Curiosity. New information. New ideas. Creativity. Opportunity. It drains our energy and our potential. It is like holding up an energetic shield against almost everything you *want*.

Of course, at times it is necessary to use our voice, to speak up about what isn't okay, or to state our preferences. But what I am saying is that we are far more likely to manifest what we want – the relationships, the career, the friends, the money – if we focus on possibility rather than why something or someone is so fundamentally wrong. I have no doubt that you will go further in life if you deal with challenging situations deftly, address people with grace and maturity, and if you approach situations with a can-do attitude.

In your heart, you don't want to see only the dark side of life, of the world, or of the people you meet on your path. In your heart, you want to experience *love*. Possibility. Divine truth. The deep purpose behind all actions, events, and moments. And in your soul, you don't truly think anything is anyone's "fault". You are wiser than that. You know there is a divine plan playing out around you 24 hours a day and that we are all part of it, without fault or flaw.

By asking ourselves what the gift, the opportunity, and the miracle in each moment is, we humble ourselves. We find the light and discover the pathway through our adversities. We connect with the universe and enrich our lives with wisdom and guidance. We remember that our lives are filled with blessings that billions of other people would want in an instant, if given the chance. And in our state of gratitude, we magnetise everything we dream of towards us: moments of authentic connection, mind-blowing synchronicity, and guidance for your path.

Even though we will encounter many moments that challenge us, we have a choice what we do with them. Will we react out of emotion? Will we complain to our friends and family about every and any little thing that bothers us? Will we post every annoyance we experience on our social media profiles, dumping our frustration into the world around us? Or will we do the best we can with what we have been given and look on the bright side of life?

You are greater than anything you may complain about. You can rise above whatever bothers you and embody a state of grace. You can shift out of victim energy and into a sage-like perspective on the circumstances in your life. You can release your attachment to discomfort, denial, and righteousness, get focused instead on the work *you* are here to do, and channel your energy into far worthier pursuits.

Don't allow relentless negativity to destroy your dreams. That only undermines your fulfilling life. Let's trade blame for a bigger game and swap dissatisfaction for a brighter future. There is so much for us to do, feel, be, achieve, and experience here in this world – and it is extraordinary. Let's not waste a minute more than is necessary complaining about he or she or they or them or this or that. Instead, let's direct our precious energy into what *gives* us energy: our mission here, the purpose that we live for, the people we love, what we love to do, our life's work on Earth.

45
Drama Addiction

"Not my circus, not my monkeys."

Polish Proverb
Quoted by my father, George Gowor

There's no question about it: drama can be addictive. What's happening in your workplace, in your friends' lives, in the news, on that binge-worthy TV show. On a very human level, we like the drama, and let's admit it, we all have nosy tendencies. *What's happening now? Ooh, did you hear about that? Look at what they are wearing, who they are dating, how much money they are making. Did you know that so-and-so cheated on so-and-so? I heard that she is getting divorced. Whoa, I can't believe they sold their house. I can't wait to see what happens next!* *Pulls out the popcorn*

Is drama and gossip entertaining? Yes, and especially in the case of movies and media, it is designed to be. But is it deeply meaningful? Rarely. And because of this, will it empower us enormously to become conscious of how often and how deeply we become caught up in it? Definitely, as there is no question that being overly entangled with what is happening in the world around us only robs us of presence and profound miracles. "He said, she said," is exhausting and it distracts us from productive action and delays us living the life we want.

Most drama isn't inspiring or uplifting or encouraging. In fact, it is quite the opposite. It is rooted in irrational emotion that drains our potential. It is filled with victim stories and exaggerations. It is shallow. It is deflating. It is noisy. And because it is so easy to become distracted or addicted to it, it takes maturity to transcend it: to close the door on it, to cut it off, to turn down the volume, to walk away. It takes wisdom to recognise when we need to break out of the gossip and start a whole new life-affirming cycle where we are far more engaged in our own lives than we are in that person's business.

It is my perspective and experience that we often become fixated on drama and engage in gossip because our own life feels empty. In other words, because we haven't figured out who we are or what we *really* want to devote our life to yet, we become obsessed with what others are doing. Because we are holding back from pursuing our purpose or going after our dreams, we seek that fulfilment around us. Because we have been too afraid to take a leap of faith and live the life that ignites us, we live vicariously through humanity.

But the pleasure that we feel when watching TV shows and talking about so-and-so and focusing on what our neighbours are doing is fleeting – and it won't ever replace the satisfaction we experience when we do what we LOVE. When we get out there and become part of the world. When we put our heart into a meaningful work we adore. When we share our gifts and make an impact. To find this fulfilment, this deep satisfaction, we must turn off the TV and disconnect from 'the feed'. We must say no to the noise.

The irony here is that *because* we sometimes use drama to numb out our emptiness, we never discover what we want and create it. We never design the blueprint for a fulfilling life and live it. We remain numb instead of awakening to the life that is possible for us, the one I firmly believe we are born for. We engage in gossip instead of silencing the noise and hearing the voice of our soul that guides us to where we were always meant to be. We become stuck in a cycle of watching others live their lives instead of living our OWN.

I promise you this: most of the drama that we allow ourselves to become caught up in is trivial. In the long run, it won't count – and believe me, you won't want to define your life by it. In most cases, it is either not *that* big of a deal or simply not our business. It can be entertaining, sure, but not fulfilling. It doesn't create nor contribute to the results we want. It doesn't move us forwards in life, change the position we are currently in, or take us to where we want to go. In fact, obsessing over drama often does the exact opposite; it keeps us stuck.

What happened in that TV show this week won't change how you feel about your own life and filling your attention span with gossip won't move you forwards on your journey. To create lasting change, you must embody a monk-like discipline: to look inwards, to reflect, to contemplate, and then answer the deeper questions about yourself and your existence. We cannot do this while constantly plugged into and drowning ourselves in drama.

Your life will *not* become empty without drama. On the contrary, it will become fuller than it ever was before. As you opt out of the drama, you will find the purpose of your life. You will connect with why you are here and what you were born to do. As you unsubscribe from the gossip feed, you will tune into an entirely different feed: the guidance and wisdom from your heart and soul.

As you empty your mind of the addictive shallow junk, it will become filled with treasure: illuminating ideas, inspired thoughts, spiritual epiphanies, awakening revelations, pure unfiltered genius, prophetic visions. You will experience new depth in your relationships, deeper rest, and a stronger connection to your SOUL.

You will become pulled into the slipstream of your purpose, encounter magic, experience synchronicities, discover new opportunities, and be able to create the empowered life that suits you perfectly. Your energy will become far more magnetic, and you *will* be more attractive. You *will* become poised and powerful.

That is what is possible when we release our desire to indulge in drama. Imagine a life that is overflowing with everything that inspires you. Imagine a life that is rich with exquisite beauty and miracles. Imagine a life that is so authentic and meaningful that you have no 'emptiness' that you would otherwise want to fill with trivial news or entertaining gossip. That is the life that you can claim with every moment that you choose to detach from drama and dive into your dharma.

46
YOUR INNER PERFECTIONIST

"Success depends on high standards, not on being flawless. The target is not perfection – it's excellence."

ADAM GRANT

It's time to call your inner perfectionist into the room and sit them down for a good talk. Is your drive for perfection helping or hindering you? Are you fiddling with your artwork endlessly without showing it to anyone? Do you practice for hours on end without ever performing? Do you keep editing that book repeatedly, thinking that it isn't done yet? Are you so afraid to let others see your creation that you never allow the world to experience what you have been working on all this time?

As one of my business mentors said in a seminar many years ago, we must balance our perfectionist with our progressionist and allow ourselves to take imperfect action. In other words, making sure that we don't become so obsessed with getting things right that we don't end up moving forwards at all. Fiddling endlessly or tweaking for days, weeks, months, or even years, might *seem* productive, but you must ask yourself: is it necessary? Or am I actually readier for the world than I realise?

There is no doubt that aiming for perfection *is* a vital ingredient of success and that having high standards for ourselves, our performance, and our results matters. In many cases, it is the stuff that the world's legends and winners and champions are made of. They care fiercely about reaching new levels, about pressing into and going beyond limits, about adding epic value, about breaking glass ceilings, and about setting new records. They care about doing the best they can or even being the best in the world at what they do. That vision and mission drives and inspires them, and you also need that fire if you are to unleash your greatness, your true capabilities.

If you are focused on progress without any consideration for perfection, you won't master your own craft – because mastery of anything *requires* a commitment to perfection. It is impossible to grow a thriving business that serves thousands of satisfied customers or rise to the top of an industry or compete with the best if you don't pay attention to the necessary details required for excellence.

That commitment, albeit intense, is vital for greatness and this is why doing what we love is vital because it carries us through the necessary effort required for excellence. I would even go so far as to say that if you don't care about doing the best you can do and pushing yourself to a new level – be it writing, dancing, boxing, selling, acting, or singing – then it is likely not your highest calling or true path in life. Why? Because when it is your purpose, the obsession to do 'better' comes naturally.

But if your perfectionistic tendencies get out of hand, you will spend forever refining and tweaking, inevitably delaying the completion, release, and sharing of your life's work. If I never published my books once I had written them, you would never read them. And so,

I can say, with hand on heart, that creating one's ripple in the world eventually requires a huge leap of faith. To let go. To surrender. To put down the tools. To hit print. To get it out there. To give people a chance to buy your product, to be blessed by your service, to experience your brilliance, to receive your wisdom, to see your performance.

The irony of being a perfectionist is two-fold. One is that the notion of perfection is rather illusive. How do we know when we have reached it? We must know what we are aiming for and what that vision of perfection looks like in order to strategically work our way towards it. If we are endlessly striving, working relentlessly, and giving ourselves harsh feedback at every turn, then we may as well give up entirely, making the attachment to producing perfection counterproductive. You must work *with* yourself if you are to do your best work.

The second irony is that when we hold such high standards on our own work and push ourselves to near-impossible standards, we forget that while we may aim for our work to be a 10 out of 10, even a 5 out of 10 is often good enough for the world around us. In other words, it doesn't necessarily *have* to be your absolute best work to change the world.

Let that sink in. In this case, maybe it's worth considering that you *are* ready. Maybe you have already produced something of great enough value to serve a million people. Maybe what you have already done and what you can do today *is* valuable enough to touch and change people's lives.

The way forwards is to balance the two: perfection and progress. It is to stand on that stage and *learn* through practice. It is to let the act of expressing your gift turn you into a master. It is to relax enough to put yourself and your work out there and to test and refine it through feedback. To set it free, give it wings, so you can watch, feel, and experience it making waves in the world.

We become great when we are doing our thing, not when we are just thinking about it. This is why dreams take a superhuman level of courage: to step up, stand out, try it, test your skills, be assessed, be liked or approved of, and *seen*. And you know what? There is no exception to that rule. It is not only unlikely but impossible that you will fulfil your purpose without using your gifts, without giving it a go, without practice, without letting go and believing in the value of what you have already produced.

This leaves you with only one thing to do: start. Do it. Try it out. Experiment. To find that fine line between "enough" and "extraordinary". To know in your heart when the work is ready. We may aim to give the best talk, do our best training session, deliver the best performance. But the truth is, there is only ever the *next* talk, the *next* training session, the *next* performance. All we can do is give it our all in each moment, knowing with peace in our heart that we are walking our path in the world, moving forward and making waves as we go.

47
FEAR

"I am not afraid. I was born to do this."

JOAN OF ARC

When I interviewed my network to ask what *they* think stops people from living their purpose, potential, and dreams, the most common answer was fear. Fear of failure, fear of success, fear of not making money, fear of the unknown – you name it. Fear seemed to be the biggest reason for people either stopping part-way through achieving a dream, or never stepping onto the field to begin with. It seems then that if we never learn to understand and manage our fear, we will never master our life.

Fear is a physical stress response that kicks in when we assume that we will experience pain – be it social pain, relationship pain, career pain, financial pain, spiritual pain, or physical pain – and our body attempts to protect us by steering us away from the potential danger. But if we live our lives being afraid of everything, living in panic, and attached to our worries, then *yes*, our fear will limit our potential and undermine our dreams.

If you are living with a patterned fear response from years of adversity, unresolved trauma, and high stress, where fear becomes the primary response to any new experience, it can consume you.

Instead of being inspired or quietly enthusiastic about your own future or the possibilities that await you, you default into expecting the worst. Instead of focusing on what you love, all your energy becomes consumed by trying to keep yourself in a bubble.

It's no way to thrive, but I also know that even if you don't feel tightly wound and terrified by all the potential hurts and pains of the world, fear will still be part of your life. In fact, the bigger your dreams, the bigger the steps and acts of courage and leaps of faith required to achieve them. This is why learning to work with our fear to expand instead of shrink our lives is profound, to say the least.

Here's how I address my own fears. First, I acknowledge the presence of the fear. Then, I calm my body down. I use whatever means necessary to let my body know that she is okay, that she is safe, and that I have her back. Alternate nostril breathing, a walk in the sun, laughter, more breathing, exercise, a hug with my man, even more deep breathing – they are equally effective for resetting the nervous system and shifting my body from a state of fight-flight into 'rest and digest' mode.

Then, I look into the core of the fear. To dissolve it, I need to know what the trigger of my fear is: what specifically is perplexing me? What am I worrying about? I quickly identify the exact issue that sent me into a panic to begin with, for example, worrying about business cash-flow or an upcoming media interview. From there, I can find a solution – a strategy to overcome my problem – and I can set it in motion.

It has taken years of practice, but I have trained myself to complete these steps as quickly as possible: to calm down, identify the source, and implement a solution. I have coached myself to breathe through it, remembering that anxiety is often an irrational projection onto the future of what I dread might occur, feedback to highlight an area where I could grow, or simply an action waiting to happen. I then *use* the energy of fear to act, rise up, and move forward. When we use this approach, fear becomes the ally, not the enemy nor a reason to sabotage everything you've ever wanted.

What we don't realise is that the majority of the things we are afraid of are a mere pimple on the landscape of our life. And yet when our survival instinct becomes triggered, it blows it heavily out of proportion. It feels impossible to look past the smaller issues, and a pothole can seem like the end of the road.

But when we relax, we can access our forebrain – the prefrontal cortex – and then, we can strategise. We can see more of the situation and can therefore access all of the information available to us. It enables us to tap into our spiritual powers: our intuition, our heart, our higher self, our soul, to guide us through. In that space, we know what to do – what next step to take – to resolve the situation or overcome the hurdle.

Calm truly is a superpower, and there is *always* something we can do to resolve the situations that worry us. If you are afraid that you won't make money from your gifts, learn business skills. Hang out with entrepreneurs. Hire a business mentor. Hustle a little harder. If you are afraid of people judging you, list out everything you think they might judge you for and *love* yourself for it so that their judgement doesn't bother you.

If you are afraid of being rejected, ditto – love yourself more than the pain of that rejection. If you are afraid of what the future might hold, deepen your spiritual connection with and extraordinary trust in *life*.

Although I have certainly had my fair share of panic-stricken moments where I worried about money or wondered if I would make it through or freaked out when launching a new course or stepping onto a bigger stage, my deepest fear is not about these. My fear is that I won't fulfil my greatest potential in life; that I will live a life void of my values, my meaning, my heart. And that fear – coupled together with the commitment I made to myself age 19, that I would do whatever it took to live an extraordinary life – has been more than enough to spur me on to tackle the other fears that stand in my way.

Instead of allowing your fear to get the better of you, live your life with resilience. Hope. Wisdom. Love. Possibility. Potential. Recognise the difference between survival fear and the fear that is triggered when we are *growing* and fulfilling our destiny.

Reserve your fear for when it is warranted – like when a bear literally runs at you, or when you know in your bones that fight or flight *is* the smartest strategy in that situation – but don't let it become the default response nor overcome the desire to achieve your dreams. A fearful life is an unfulfilling life. So, don't become so busy trying to protect yourself from everything that might possibly hurt that you never get busy living.

48
Disconnection From Humanity

"What we do for ourselves dies with us; what we do for others remains and is immortal."

ALBERT PIKE

In 2010, I was travelling from Canada to Australia. On my way, I stopped in to visit a dear friend of mine in Los Angeles. During my visit, I seized the opportunity to tick an item off my bucket list: visiting the world-famous Agape church that was founded by Michael Bernard Beckwith, one of the stars of the self-help sensation, *The Secret*.

I sat in the chapel and listened to an inspiring sermon delivered by one of the pastors. He told a story about a time in his life when he was struggling and nothing seemed to be going well. He was experiencing a series of seemingly insurmountable personal problems and things appeared to be falling apart around him.

Then, in the midst of his angst when he was battling with many difficulties, he was offered the opportunity to be a volunteer on a two-week program to support young adults who were facing hardship. When he came home from the fortnight of volunteer work, he had an epiphany: his problems seemed to have vanished. In fact, he could barely remember what many of them were. He had learned a powerful lesson about how focusing *beyond* ourselves on what we can do for the world around us can transform our life.

This may be a reason that you are not thriving in your life right now: you are a little too focused on your own problems and not enough on the service you can deliver to humanity using your gifts. When our focus becomes too insular and self-oriented, we disconnect ourselves from the world around us. In doing so, we don't access the connections and relationships that can bring so much into our lives, from income to inspiration. This often causes us to feel stuck and lonely.

Living in service of a cause beyond us or a mission that ignites us is what helps us to overcome this. When we focus on who we could be and what we could do for the world around us, it supports us to find our higher purpose. It provides us with the feeling of being needed and a reason to excel. This deep meaning pulls us through extraordinary suffering. It helps us to put the pains and challenges of our human life in context of something greater and ironically, it helps us to solve the problems we were worried about to begin with.

Thriving careers, businesses, and legacies are born out of service, from a desire to solve a problem, to lift a burden, to find a solution, to share a creation. They involve a deeply personal desire to stand for a cause, to provide what is needed, to share what can make a difference – and in every instance of extraordinary careers and empires, there is a service beyond the self. There is a desire to make a difference as well as an income and a legacy as well as a life.

I am not referring to being overly focused on yourself in the sense that you think you are better than everyone else, but more so that your dominant focus is on you OVER others rather than you AND others. When your own struggle is the only thing on your mind, you can easily forget about the impact you could have on the world around you. This can cause you to miss out on the extraordinary and life-changing experience of serving others: of putting your heart, mind, and soul to work and using what you have within you.

Being connected to humanity and living a life of service doesn't mean forgetting yourself completely, sacrificing everything for others, or neglecting your desires and needs – not at all. It is about the beauty, the healing, the love, the blessings that flood into your life when you become part of the world around you rather than struggling endlessly in the world within you. These are the gifts we discover when we look outside of ourselves and discover our role as part of humanity: what we could do with our life that would have great meaning.

There is also a vital link to be made between confidence and service. When you are perpetually focused on yourself, it is easy to beat yourself up and focus on your apparent flaws. You look at your body, your behaviours, your past, your habits, your education (or lack thereof), or your bank account, and you can find a million shortcomings. You compare yourself to others, pick yourself apart, and measure, measure, measure.

But when you focus *beyond* yourself, you turn your attention and energy to how you can use what is within you to serve those around you.

Then, it is no longer about you, the seemingly flawed and insignificant human flying on a rock through space. It is about the person you are in service of: the customer, the person buying your product, the client you are helping, the person you are assisting.

It is there that you transcend your human insecurities and unleash what you are made of. Potential. Power. Giftedness. You see what you can do to help, touch, move, and inspire others and in doing so, your life feels and becomes that much more significant. You free yourself from the endless list of doubts and judgements you have about yourself. Then, you can begin to see yourself as your loved ones, as your clients, and as God sees you.

This is how we experience deep, deep love. The sense of belonging, the feeling of being appreciated, the experience of being welcomed, knowing we are needed: we all seek. Your life takes on a whole new level of depth and meaning as you fulfil a life of expressing yourself, rather than beating down on yourself.

That is the power of looking, working, feeling, and living in service. It helps us to transcend our personal suffering, touch our greatness with our very own hands, witness our innate magnificence, and turn our world into high-definition colour. The simple moral of this is to live our lives *with* others, instead of living our lives solely focused on ourselves in our own little world. As my beautiful mother said to me, "We are not here alone and there is a beautiful world out there."

49
Image Insecurities

"Mother Teresa didn't walk around complaining about her thighs. She had sh*t to do."

Sarah Silverman

It's time for a moment of sheer vulnerability and raw, unfiltered personal honesty: my body image issues have affected my life and dreams. Tracing back through the years, I can see how insecure I have felt physically at times, for my hair, my nose, my weight, and my general level of attractiveness. The truth is that, even now, as I write this book, I sometimes feel quite uncomfortable in my own skin.

Despite having been called "beautiful" or "gorgeous" on many occasions (and never struggling to attract a good-looking partner either!), my body image issues have certainly caused me to hold back from certain opportunities I would love to pursue. On occasion, I still feel quite self-conscious when people look at me, when I am on video, or even when I am just out and about in a shopping centre.

It is not a constant feeling that I never escape from. There have certainly been several moments in my life where I embraced my body, celebrated my unique beauty, and felt confident, sexy, or attractive – but I have also experienced many moments where I felt a sudden desire for the floor to open up so I could vanish.

Image Insecurities

It's unfortunate how we can let our external appearance determine the life we live or why not being 'model hot' can cause us to withdraw from the world instead of leap into the limelight – but it happens often. So many of us experience it, basing our self-worth on how we look more than who we are and what we do.

Unrealistic ideals and expectations are typically the culprit of image insecurities. Photoshopped magazine pictures, filtered social media images, and the people devoted to beauty and fitness in the world can sneak up on us subconsciously and trigger shame or comparison. This can be exacerbated by any comments we have received in the past about our appearance, even if they were made in jest by a loved one or even by someone you don't care much for, like a stranger on the internet.

All of the above creates the notion that your life would be somehow better if you had a different face, different nose, bigger breasts, smaller butt, slender waist, chiselled jaw. Wishing we were more physically attractive can plague us and, if we don't seek to heal the wounding, our shallow perceptions of our own body WILL sabotage our greatest aspirations.

Our body can seem permanent and unchangeable – and in many ways it is. We journey with it for our entire life, from when we arrive here to the day we draw our final breath. You exist within your body in every single second of your life, and judging it because of certain parts is only going to cause friction and rob you of the joy and fulfilment that is possible for you.

Pursuing my purpose has been by far the most powerful antidote to this ongoing internal battle. My love of what I do, my determination to share my message, and my calling to inspire people to reach for more has empowered me to push forwards regardless of my body insecurities. On so many occasions, my spiritual calling has *moved* me to go on television, be photographed, speak up in public, lead global projects, and stand on stages – because I feel *compelled* to… and any personal feelings about my body, my arms, my height weren't going to stop me from that.

In pursuing my purpose, I discovered that following my authentic path in this world is in itself a deep source of charisma, radiance, and beauty. When you do what you love, your body becomes ignited by an energy far *beyond* the body; your soul. In those moments, you GLOW. The light shines from inside you and it alters your being from within. Your body *will* look and feel more attractive – to yourself and the world around you – when you are moved by the love and vision within you.

In my exploration to start dismantling this inner obstacle, I also had to ask myself honestly, 'Has my body *really* stopped me from living the life I want?' The simple answer is "No." In fact, my body has made *everything* possible. From travelling the world to mentoring clients to running my company to making love to writing this very book, my body has not prevented but rather enabled the life I dream of (that brings tears to my eyes). She is a miracle – and in this awareness, it feels trivial to ever doubt her beauty. She gave me LIFE. This life. The one I love.

Upgrading my wardrobe, having my colours done with a stylist, and learning about inner wellness have helped greatly on the journey of finding confidence and empowerment in myself. But I know that the real work has been, and is, in simply loving my body for all she is and is not, for where she is and how she is in, in all the years of my time here. No number of compliments or contrary opinions from the outside can change that inner perception until I do it from within.

So, after bearing my naked truth about my own body image (see what I did there?), reflect on this for yourself. Are your physical insecurities getting in the way of what your soul guides you to do? Do you love the skin you are in? What parts of your physical self could you love more? How can you empower your health, beauty, and fitness to make the most of what you've been given while also loving yourself, exactly as you are in this very moment?

Perhaps it is time to consider that we were born with the perfect body for our mission here on Earth and to give thanks for this extraordinary creature our souls are inhabiting for a lifetime. Perhaps it is time for us to recognise and appreciate our appearance while remembering we are far deeper and extraordinary than we might feel when we look in the mirror or see ourselves in photographs. And perhaps it is time to *embrace* ourselves on all levels – body, mind, heart, and soul – and love our body for the incredible instrument it is.

Wherever you want to go, your body will take you there. Whatever you dream of achieving, your body will be your vehicle. In every twist, turn, and stage of your life journey, your body will be with you. It loves you, and as you give yourself permission to do what you love and live out the dreams inside your heart, your body will come to life like never before – and you WILL accept and love yourself for all that you are. You will love your body for all it is and isn't, and never again will you let image insecurities be the cause of you having less than you desire.

50
HUGGING THE ROCK

"The greatness of a man's power is the measure of his surrender."
WILLIAM BOOTH

This topic is about how we hold onto the things that cause unnecessary hardship in our life. It is about the way we refuse to let go of the things that make us suffer, the areas where we make things more painful or difficult than they have to be, and the ways in which we sabotage ourselves and the life we yearn for by doing it the hard way. This is the ultimate self-sabotage: where we resist support and create resistance that costs us progress, growth, and fulfilment. I call this 'hugging the rock'.

It all boils down to this one essential question: are you working *with* or *against* yourself to achieve what you want? If you resent yourself, you will criticise yourself, judge yourself, and label yourself unfairly. If you beat yourself up, you will hold yourself back, get caught up on tangents, attract even more obstacles, and waste time. You will stay stuck in the rut instead of finding the smoother road. You won't allow life to lift and guide you to where you wish to be.

But if you *believe* in yourself, bet on yourself, and love yourself relentlessly, you will find your flow. You will experience a deep harmony with yourself and your journey. You will encourage yourself, reach out, get help, look for a better way, and attract miracles. You will feel guided, determined, persistent, strong, and humble on *your* path.

It is impossible to achieve your dreams if you feel that you don't deserve them or to create the life you want if you are unconsciously causing chaos in your world because you have got a vendetta against yourself. We cannot punish ourselves and perform optimally at the same time. Our dreams, especially the grandest ones, require deep alignment, self-respect, and self-love. Believing that you haven't earned your dreams unless absolutely everything has been impossible, draining, or difficult will break you in the end – because you also need ease, flow, support, and grace to flourish. We all do.

No legend, from celebrities to world leaders, ever reached the top by beating themselves into the ground endlessly. Even though they worked hard for their accomplishments, deep down, they believed they were born for greater things. They believed they had a higher destiny, and they allowed themselves to rise to it. They *allowed* themselves to do what they love, to make their mark, to achieve what they dream.

There is a difference between tackling worthy challenges and punishing yourself by making things difficult or complicated. There is a difference between testing your limits to unleash your hidden capabilities and taking on so much that it causes burnout or breakdown. Wisdom is knowing the difference, and self-love is giving up the pattern of holding onto what holds us back and weighs us down.

What difficulty are you holding onto today? Is it doing that task in your business, even though hiring someone else to do it would free you up to grow your business exponentially? Is it thinking that you must do all the housework yourself when you barely have time for it? Is it keeping that friendship alive, even though you feel drained whenever their name appears in your inbox? Is it trying to work it out yourself instead of hiring a mentor? Or is it undercharging for your services, your time, your value?

Study your life carefully and find those areas where you tend to feel consistently stuck: areas where you often feel weighed down, frustrated, lost, or confused. If you have been feeling stuck there for more than three months, or even three weeks, it might indicate that you are holding onto a rock that is weighing you down and causing your life to feel like a constant uphill climb.

Where are you being stubborn and doing things the hard way? In what area are you working harder than is required or using *too* much of your energy to get something done? Why do you make things trickier than they either have to be or could be? Are you punishing yourself for something and so you make achieving what you want ten times harder? Do you not feel worthy of your heart's desires and so you avoid letting your problems be solved? What is it *really* about?

Regardless of *why* you are carrying those boulders, perhaps it is time to drop the rock. It's time to stop hating on yourself and surrender what causes suffering in your life. It is time to let that which no longer serves you, and that which drowns you, simply fall away. It is time to let the light shine in the areas of your life that are currently shrouded in darkness… to allow yourself to be supported, accept the love you are worthy of, and find your way through to the other side.

The relief that will flood into your life when you finally, finally let go of what has been holding you back and weighing you down will be immense. You will feel like yourself again. You will recover from burnout and say goodbye to overwhelm for good. You will find the energy to do the things you have always dreamed of, that which you have wanted to do for so long but were too busy to pursue. In releasing what you do not want, you will make room for what lights you up to flourish.

Gone will be the days where you break apart under stress, where you frustrate against life, and where you wonder why you can't figure it all out. In its place will be days where things flow, where you do what you love, and where you radiate your heart to those around you. In dropping the rock, your power and beauty will emerge, and the world will get the best of you. It is there and then that you will rise up and fulfil your destiny; that you will live the life you dream of, the one you were born for.

You don't need to prove anything to anyone by doing things tough. You have already shown yourself that you are strong beyond all previous notions. So now, it is time to release your grip on what causes pain and open your arms to life. Let that issue resolve itself, that question answer itself, and that perfect person show up, so that you can get on with far bigger and better things. It's your destiny.

51
LOW VIBRATION LIVING

"Everything is energy. Match the frequency of the reality you want and you cannot help but get that reality. It can be no other way. This is not philosophy. This is physics."

ALBERT EINSTEIN

On both a spiritual and scientific level, you are vibrational in nature. You resonate at different frequencies throughout your life and are simultaneously affected by the vibration of everything that you encounter. Every person, place, object, experience, feeling, thought, idea, and situation has both a vibrational essence and an energy that it radiates to the world around it.

The vibration will either feel high, clear, and light, or it will feel heavy, dense, and draining. It will either inspire you or depress you. It will either open your mind and heart or close them. It either enhances your life force or depletes it. Every single thing that you experience, think, and feel throughout your life resonates somewhere on the scale.

The power within this truth is that we can *use* vibration to shift ourselves and our lives and create the future we desire. How? By surrounding ourselves with higher vibration people and places, by immersing ourselves in inspiring tasks, by filling our days with that which lifts our energy – and by being disciplined about doing so.

This journey starts with your own vibration. Here's what tends to lower your personal vibration: junk food, mainstream media, clothes that you don't love, 12,000 unread emails, overeating, a lack of exercise, victim stories, trashy TV shows, lack of spontaneity, excessive alcohol or drugs, living by others' opinions, uninspiring relationships, unhelpful conversations, and holding onto your own emotions. These may be generalisations, but you get my drift.

Now here is what tends to transform and supercharge your personal vibration: daily movement, regular mindset work, emotional healing, education, mentors, investing in yourself, travelling, hydration, clean eating, alternative wellness, loving yourself unconditionally, stretching, respecting your needs and wants, spiritual reflection, downtime, productive time, organising your life, and doing what you love.

A person who does all of *these* things is a powerhouse – a force to be reckoned with – and they are far more likely to achieve and fulfil their true potential as a by-product of their personal mastery. They are clear-minded, open-hearted, and high-spirited. It is a truly extraordinary goal that we can all aim for.

As you raise your own vibration, you can then start to shift and raise the vibration of your life. The approach to raising the vibration of your *life* is two-fold. First, remove and minimise anything that feels dense and draining. This might be projects, commitments, or friendships that you have outgrown. Relationships that have run their course. Or even your job.

Then, allow yourself to withdraw from those situations that no longer serve you. This might not be an easy journey or a quick process in some situations. It might involve extensive paperwork or divorce or closing an entire part of your business, but regardless of the effort required, it will be worth it, every time.

Second, bring in higher vibration by literally surrounding yourself with it. Spend time in environments that ignite and uplift you, whether that is nature to refresh your mind or cafés that inspire your thoughts. Make time for conversations with like-minded people. Be choosy about where you go, what you do, and who you do it with. Fill your personal space – home, bedroom, office, car – with what you *love*. It will transform the underlying energy of your life from one of confusion or heaviness to one of lightness and inspiration.

In doing all of the above, you will experience a higher frequency of inspiring moments. You will become a magnet for epic ideas and life-changing insights. Your life will start to feel extraordinary, even when you are tackling mundane tasks. And you will be empowered to heal and transcend that which has weighed you down or held you back.

Train yourself to feel the vibration of who you are, what you do, what you say, and what and who is around you. Be present and tune in. How does it feel? What does it move or stir in you? Does it uplift you? Does it bring you closer to or further away from what you dream of? What impact does it have on your mood? Your energy? Your mind? Your body? Trust what you feel, for your intuitive guidance is rarely wrong.

The older I get, the more fixated I am on what is and feels wholesome. This shift inside my heart occurred after my father passed away and I encountered the humbling realisation of just how many trivial things simply don't and won't matter in the end. I am not just interested in filling every inch of my life with that which is higher vibration in nature; I am devoted to it.

As the years pass, I am far less interested in small talk, popular opinion, gossip, or watching other people live their lives on social media. I want to spend my time in deep conversation, mastering my craft, experiencing quality downtime, exploring nature, having inspiring adventures, and listening to my soul. I want to minimise my time caught in emotions or judgements and maximise my time doing what I love and spending it with who I love.

I want to focus on meaningful pursuits and prioritise only the work that moves and matters. I want to leave a legacy, be lit up on a soul level, and live my dream NOW – and I want that for my friends, my customers, my readers, and my loved ones. I want it for you: a life filled with love. Beauty. Wisdom. Freedom. Inspiration. Flow. Revelation. Healing. Growth. What a life that will be. You need that if you are to fulfil the dreams inside your heart and express the gifts, the talents, and the potential you were born with.

Immerse yourself in the vibrations of love, gratitude, and inspiration as often as possible. Seek clarity and certainty. Eliminate anything that pulls you out of the flow. Low-vibration foods, habits, places, emotions, and conversations will only detract away from what you truly want. One by one, they will pull you away from the experience of life that is possible for you, but high vibrations will be the air beneath your wings and carry you to great places.

52
DELAYING YOUR DREAMS

"Fortune favours the brave."

VIRGIL

Thinking that we have still got time is one of the greatest downfalls of being alive and human, and it is one of the simplest yet most serious reasons why so many don't live the life they want. So often, we don't realise or comprehend how crucially valuable every day is and so we take our time for granted, thinking that our goals won't take *that* long to achieve, or that we can put off what matters to us until later. But before we know it, our time is running out.

Unfortunately, most of us get caught out by this at least once in our lifetime. It sneaks up on us like a ninja in the night and then one day, it hits us: *I'm running out of time. My life is not as long as I thought it would be. I really won't live forever. I still haven't done the things I dream of. There are so many places I still want to visit. Where did that week go? Oh God, I'm turning 50 this year.*

Those moments are humbling to say the least, when we realise that a year or years or a decade has passed, and we still haven't acted on that idea. That we dream of being on stage, but we haven't begun practising yet. That we still want to write that book, but we haven't started. That we knew what we wanted to do when we grew up, and now we are nearly 40 and we still haven't done it. These are the moments when our immortal self – our dreamer, our thinker, our creator – comes face-to-face with the mortal reality of time.

These brutal moments of revelation are a wake-up call; where we realise that we must run our life instead of letting it run us if we are to have a chance at fulfilment. We must do what we can to live from our expanded self instead of being weighed down by our human challenges. We must deftly conquer our internal, external, mental, emotional, physical obstacles. We must discover our purpose so we can spend less time wondering what it is and more time fulfilling it. These moments are therefore a nudge from deep, deep within you to get in gear and get going on your path of destiny.

Regardless of whether taking our time for granted is because we are too caught up in what feels urgent today, too focused up in our emotions or too distracted by what others think of who we are and what we do, it is up to us to change it. To interrupt the pattern of delaying what matters. To take a pause, a long moment, a week off, a month off to slow down and ask ourselves: what would I love to do with my life? What is *really* holding me back and how can I overcome it? What plan can I put into place to achieve my wildest dreams?

We all say this as we age, that time seems to fly by faster the older we get. Once we reach 30, a year doesn't feel like forever like it did when we were young. A week feels like a day, months slip by with lightning speed, and suddenly it's Christmas again. If we are not living fully each day by choosing our course, by setting our goals, by stepping up fearlessly, then we only compound the feeling that we are not making the most of our life as we age… because, perhaps, it is true.

The Life You Dream Of

This is why the importance of doing what we dream of only grows with time. We must overcome the inertia of time, of growing older, of dealing with adult responsibilities, of living in a fast-paced world. It is up to us to make the conscious and concerted effort to be present in each and every precious second of our time here.

To realise that this moment – right here and right now – is so sacred that it only happens once. To push aside the trivial for good. To recognise the opportunity and the blessing of each minute – and embrace it. And to harness our courage for every action required to LIVE and LOVE an extraordinary future.

You came to Earth for a reason: what was it? I firmly believe that you chose to be here – in this body, in this country, in this culture, and in this time in history – and that you have a mission to fulfil on the planet, be it local or global. There is no mistake about this, and the world needs you to fulfil the vision and the mission that is inside your heart.

So, here is your reminder – this IS the moment. Now IS the time. Today IS the day – and it is a gift. So, stop pushing what you would love to do today into tomorrow or delaying today's calling into next year. Don't leave it unsaid, unfelt, ignored, sidelined, undone, incomplete, unexpressed. Get to work on what matters. Find your focus and get moving. Use the energy you have for the goals that fire you up, for the cause you care about, and for the path you feel moved to walk down. Lean in and live deeply.

Don't wait for the love you seek; find and feel it now. Enough holding back from what you feel called to say and do. Enough of waiting for the right time to make a move. Enough doubts, fears, worries, hesitation, distraction, procrastination. Stop saying IF and start saying WHEN to your dreams. No, you won't achieve it overnight, but if you show up daily for your purpose, you *will* move forwards and then, when your time is eventually up, you will die knowing that you made the absolute most of it all.

Live openly with curiosity, fire, and determination, ignited by the vision, the dream, inside your heart. Let it guide you in each moment – and never give up on your calling. Allow your heartfelt mission and purpose to be greater than anything that can, could, or would otherwise undermine your magnificent existence. It is time to do what you were born for, step up, stand out, and close the gap between where you are and where you want to be.

Your Reflection Time

We have taken a deep, deep journey of self-reflection and inner exploration together in this book as I have shared 52 reasons why I believe that people hold back from their potential, purpose, and dreams in life.

Now, I want to give you the opportunity to add your own.

Your growth path is unique, and I know that the topic of unlocking your power and fulfilling your heartfelt aspirations is deeply personal. I also know that there are many more causes of an unfulfilling existence that I haven't covered in this book.

This is why in the coming pages, you will find a blank section ready for *you* to fill in. My invitation is for you to reflect even more deeply on your own life and then ask yourself:

What do I feel *truly* holds me back from the life I want?
Why have I *really* not achieved what I dream of yet?

I will guide you through the process of exploring this 'reason' with journal prompts. On the next page, you will also find a list of other potential reasons that may resonate with you and that you might choose to write about for yourself.

Don't be shy about writing in the book (it is a compliment to me as the author if you do!) but if you do wish to keep your reflections to yourself, feel free to write your discoveries in a private journal instead. Either way, I understand.

If you feel inspired to share what *you* feel has held you back (or you want to share what you have broken through that changed your life), I would love to hear from you. Take a moment to send an email to info@emilygowor.com with the subject line "The Life I Dream Of" and fill me in (no spam please!).

Let's dive in.

Here is a list of other potential 'reasons' you may not have or may not be fulfilling your purpose, potential, and dreams in life.

Use these as inspiration for your own reflection.

- Religious upbringing
- Busy raising a family
- Lacking the right education
- Parental restrictions
- Physical disability or disease
- Cultural expectations
- Being close-minded
- Lacking a sense of adventure
- Fear of putting yourself out there
- Putting your partner first

Now it's your turn to write!

Use the following pages to explore. The goal is to get clear on what has held you back and to awaken a revelation about what you can do to unleash your power and reach a whole new level of your life.

You deserve it.

53:_____

Explain this reason below. Why do you feel that you aren't fulfilling or haven't fulfilled your purpose, potential, and dreams yet? How has this shown up in your life?

_____
_____
_____
_____
_____
_____
_____

What caused it? Where did it start in your journey?

_____
_____

The Life You Dream Of

What has the impact of this been? In what way do you perceive it has held you back or undermined your potential?

What is beyond this limitation? What would you love instead?

What can or could you do to overcome and transcend this?

Do you feel this limitation has run its course in your life? Are you ready to go beyond it?

Create Your Breakthrough Plan

It's time to summarise and prioritise what you feel are or have been the greatest 'blocks' that limit your potential and therefore, your life. We will do this in three steps:

1. **Review all the topics in the book, including the one that you added at the end.**

2. **Write a list over the page of the reasons you resonated with that feel like they could be blocking your purpose, potential, and dreams. For example, time management or approval addiction.**

   This will form a personal summary of the biggest reasons *you* feel you haven't been making the absolute most out of your life.

   Remember, by clearly identifying and naming your invisible limits, you can find a way to break through, dissolve, or overcome them and greet the life that is waiting for you on the other side (and it truly is).

The Life You Dream Of

- _____
- _____
- _____
- _____
- _____
- _____
- _____
- _____
- _____
- _____
- _____
- _____
- _____
- _____
- _____
- _____
- _____
- _____
- _____

Create Your Breakthrough Plan

3. Now, review your list above. Choose the top three that you feel are holding you back the most and rewrite them on the lines below.

This will help you to prioritise the main areas to transform first that will make the biggest difference in your life.

1. _____

2. _____

3. _____

You CAN do this.

Conclusion

"What is there to fight for? Everything!
Life itself, isn't that enough?
To be lived, suffered, enjoyed!
What is there to fight for?
Life is a beautiful, magnificent thing, even to a jellyfish.
What is there to fight for?
The trouble is, you won't fight!
You've given in, continually dwelling on sickness and death.
But there's something just as inevitable as death - and that's life.
Life, life, life!
Think of the power that's in the universe, moving the Earth, growing the trees.
And that's the same power within you if you'll only have the courage and the will to use it."

Charlie Chaplin

When I was just 19 years old, I thought about ending my life. I had dropped out of my university degree a year earlier and I was depressed. Feeling lost and worthless, I had no idea how I was going to move forward, let alone create a future that inspired me. One night, I was driving up the highway into the city of Brisbane. Driving at 80kmph, I considered running my car into the concrete barrier that separated the lanes of traffic.

In that moment of angst when I wanted to give up completely, I felt something deep inside me that stopped me. It was an overwhelming sense of, "You're not done yet." – and that is when I knew. I knew that it wasn't my time to go, even though I had hit rock-bottom. I knew that I wanted more from my life, not to give up on it entirely. And I knew that there was so much that this world could offer me – and that moment saved me.

Although I felt daunted by the apparent distance between where I was and where I wanted to be, the decision had been made: I would make the most of my life. And once I made that decision, the universe conspired to help me to move towards the life I believe I was always destined for.

As I reflect today, there is no doubt in my mind that connecting with my soulful purpose is what pulled me through the darkness. By remembering who I was, what I loved, and why I felt I was born – to write – I found an endless source of hope, love, and healing. It became my guiding light, pulling me first through depression and then through a series of subsequent challenges involved in creating the life I love, from relationship break-ups to business difficulties and the death of my father.

Above all else, I believe deeply that discovering and pursuing our purpose is the antidote to these 52 reasons that people so often and so unfortunately do *not* live a life they love. Our calling gives us a direct connection to the source: to the light, the force, and the energy that created us. And it is this very relationship with the higher, spiritual, and all-powerful aspect of ourselves that we can transcend the most difficult of our obstacles and the deepest struggle of being human.

We *need* our purpose if we are to move forward. To shine. To flourish. To lead. To influence. To radiate. It is the healing remedy that soothes our wounds, the spark that lifts us up when we feel down, and the light at the end of the tunnel. It gives us meaning, confidence, and a reason to apply ourselves in this life; to do everything that we can with everything we have, to express our authentic selves, and to make our mark on humanity.

By doing what we love, what inspires us, we tap into resilience, far beyond anything we ever knew we had. The deep love we feel for our mission, the love we feel for our calling, and the love we experience when we express the talents we were blessed with; that is where the power to transform our life exists. I am sure that the discovery and pursuit of your purpose will do for you what mine did for me and lead you to an entirely different life.

Deep inside your heart, you believe in this greater life for yourself. You believe in a life that is filled with meaning and overflowing with fulfilment. A life where you live with your heart open and set yourself and your gifts free. A life where you devote yourself to your dharma. A life where you experience *all* of the blessings and miracles and adventures and mind-blowing, awe-inspiring moments that are available to you.

You were born for it – and every day of your life, you are being called towards it. You yearn for it. Your heart and soul are trying to pull you towards it in every moment. In every moment your heart beats, it guides you to what you love. In every moment you breathe, your soul watches over you, nudging you to lean in and create an extraordinary life – YOUR extraordinary life.

That deep-seated belief in a greater life is why you read this book. It's why you keep searching, even when the answers don't seem apparent. It's why you keep pressing forwards on your path, one step at a time, even when results feel like they are a million miles away. And it's why you never give up, even when you feel down and out, beaten up and broken open, defeated and depressed, stressed and stuck.

Because you know at your core that you weren't born for work without heart, for years without depth, for an existence without inspiration. You weren't born to suffer, to struggle, to flail, or to fall apart. You were born to RISE. To beat down the demons that bother you, to make peace with the past, to seize each moment and the opportunity of life itself and do your absolute most with it.

I believe that it is our destiny, and therefore our mission, to break down and break through every single thing – wounding, limits, and excuses – that block our purpose, potential, and dreams. That it is our greatest obligation, to ourselves and to the world around us, to get out of our own way and live a GREATER life. To discover what we are TRULY here for, to get clear on what matters and release all else, to thrive so that you can be the inspiration this world needs.

You can do this by getting quiet within yourself, feeling deeply, and allowing your calling to be heard. By dreaming (much bigger) for your future, your professional path, and your personal life. And by taking action with faith, trusting that you are being guided and that you *do* know which step to take next to fulfil your destiny here.

On your journey, you must remember that it is often *when* you pursue your purpose, your meaningful goals, and your heartfelt dreams that your limitations will come to the surface. This occurs because you are reaching for something bigger and that requires you to let go of or resolve anything that interferes with the manifestation of what you desire. Therefore, experiencing resistance is a sign of aspiration, of growth, and of expansion.

So, although facing your 'stuff' as you work towards your vision may feel defeating, you must remember that your 'blocks' bubble up not to stop you, but rather to set you free so you can go beyond them. It is by being relentless and quietly persistent in healing the human wounding that shrouds the light of your soul that you can manifest the career, the life, the legacy within you – and be an example to those around you that life doesn't have to be constant misery.

Who you are sets an example. How you live sets an example. What you do sets an example. What you achieve sets an example. Let it be one of LOVE. STRENGTH. RESILIENCE. PERSONAL POWER. BELIEF. SURRENDER. COURAGE. HUMBLENESS. Be the risk-taker for a vision you can see. Be the voice in the silence. Be the light in the darkness. Be the love the world needs.

Give yourself the life you dream of – because you want it. Do what you can do with everything you have – because you are capable of more. And reach your greatest success – because you deserve to. Do it for yourself – and do it for humanity. Do it because you refuse to believe that we are here to settle for emptiness. Do it because you believe in a vision that others can't see. Do it because you are filled with love and because you don't want to hold back what you feel compelled, driven, and inspired to do. And do it because you can't see yourself living life any other way.

In late January of 2022, I had the very last conversation with my father. Having been sick for many years, he was in the palliative care wing of the Byron Bay Hospital in New South Wales. Just six days before he died, I had called the hospital to speak to him – and it was one of the most humbling conversations of my entire life. He was heavily sedated on morphine for the pain, but in between him floating in and out of consciousness, we shared an exchange that will stay with me for the rest of my life.

During our phone call, he said to me, "My body feels like it is failing me." I said, "Dad, your body has been falling apart for 12 years." He responded, "It feels like it has been three days." This comment on its own was a confronting message about just how short and fast our lives truly are. But then he asked me, "What did I really achieve and do with my life?" I responded with a list of all the things that I had seen him do in his time here, from building houses to raising his two children. "Hmph," was his reply as he took it all in.

After a moment of silence, he then asked me, "But what did I do for myself?" Without hesitation, I said, "You did some damn good fishing, Dad!" and we both laughed. I was acutely aware in that moment that I was helping this man – the man that I had loved throughout every second of my life and more than words can possibly describe – to make peace with all that his life had and had not been. I told him, "It's okay to let go now."

Then I felt guided to ask him one final powerful question: "What would you have done with more time anyway, Dad?" His response broke my heart wide open and brought me to my knees. "I would have spent more time with my children." Four days later, I travelled interstate to visit him in the hospital and sat by his side for two hours holding his hand while he slept… and two days after that, he was gone. I was the last person to sit with him before he passed away at 5:50am on Sunday 30th January 2022.

The impact that his passing has had on my life is immeasurable, and in many ways, it is the reason that I wrote this very book; to plead to you not to wait until you've got no time left to do what is inside your heart and to make the very most of this life while you have it. What are we here for if we don't honour what we love and spend our time with who we love? It doesn't matter where you start from, it just matters where you are going and how openly you allow your love and God to direct your path.

That conversation and those final, infinitely precious moments with my dad have been a continual reminder for me of the true purpose of life and an intense motivation to transcend any and every obstacle – both those within me and those around me – that interferes with my dream. And *that* is what this book and my life's work on Earth is about: getting beyond what keeps us stuck and holds us back so we can fly. I know in my heart that my father watches over me every day and that he would be overjoyed to know that I have been writing. Dad, this one is for you.

So, please know that no matter where you are or how you feel today, that you *can* do this, and it's time to believe that each and every thing in your life is conspiring for you to achieve your wildest dreams; to unleash the potential that you were born with and to create a massive ripple in this world by being the fullest expression of your authentic self.

George Gowor

21-10-1949 - 30-1-2022

Fly free, papa

Daydream

When we were kids in the backyard,
Playing astronauts and rockstars,
No one told us to stop it,
Called us unrealistic.

Then suddenly, you're eighteen
Go to college for your plan B
What you want is too risky
Live for weekends and whiskey

We all got these big ideas
One day, they're replaced with fears
How did we get here?

Darlin', don't quit your daydream
It's your life that you're making
It ain't big enough if it doesn't scare the hell out of you
If it makes you nervous
It's probably worth it
Why save it for sleep when you could be living your daydream?

Thirty-one, waiting tables
She has the voice of an angel
Out of money and power
She only sings in the shower

All these things we say we'll get to
Shot down by the reasons not to

Darlin', don't quit your daydream
It's your life that you're making
It ain't big enough if it doesn't scare the hell out of you
If it makes you nervous
It's probably worth it
Why save it for sleep when you could be living your daydream?

So scared of failure that we fail to try
Turnin' around before the finish line
Gotta fall for a minute before you can fly

So daydream
Darlin', don't quit your daydream
It's your life that you're making
It ain't big enough if it doesn't scare the hell out of you
If it makes you nervous
It's probably worth it
Why save it for sleep when you could be living your daydream?
Why save it for sleep when you could be living your daydream?

Lyrics of *Daydream*
Lily Meola

Acknowledgements

Firstly, I would love to thank the extraordinary women of the Global Women Empowerment TV Show, Channel 31 in Melbourne, Australia. My experience of travelling to Melbourne for the interview in early 2024 and the experience of being on the show with you inspired me to start writing my next book.

The next morning after being in the studio with a group of powerful women, I sat down to write at the Grand Hyatt. The words began pouring out of me… and now here we are, celebrating the publication of my 13th book. Thank you for being a catalyst for my next literary masterpiece.

Thank you to my late father George Gowor for recognising and encouraging my writing potential when I was a teenager, and to my mother Mama Rae (Rae Antony) for being right by my side in not only the twists and turns of my life, but in the birthing of so many of my books. I would not be here without you both and I am certain I would not be the woman I am today had you not been my parents. You instilled within me a work ethic and the belief that I was born with greatness inside of me – two very precious parts of me. I love you both.

Thank you to my partner, Michael Bromley, for endlessly supporting and encouraging me on my path of dharma in this world. Thank you for providing a home space and a safe space for me to slow my life down, to heal, to simplify my work, and to do what I love: write. I love you so deeply and my gratitude is immense.

Acknowledgements

To my friend and soul brother, Codey Orgill: thank you for cheering me on during the writing of this book – and for being the inspiration for a handful of my topics. Your questions, curiosity, and support have been immeasurably valuable. You bring joy and company to my life, and you will forever hold a special place in my heart. Your presence is a blessing to this world.

To my long-time mentor and guide, Dr John F Demartini, for his life-changing work and method, The Demartini Method®. Your profound method and teachings help me to access the place beyond words where my writings flow from: my heart and soul. Thank you for your devotion to be who you are and to do what you dream so that I can do what I dream and inspire others.

To my girlfriend Enette Pauzé for the soul journey we have shared over the past two decades. Our relationship and journey is far more precious than words can express. Thank you for igniting my soul, my spark, and my fire. I will love you forever.

To my dear soul sister, Elina Passant. Your incredible persistence amidst your battles with Ehlers-Danlos Syndrome and your extraordinary spirit *inspires* me endlessly. You are a true shining example of how our soul's purpose can inspire and guide us through our adversities on Earth.

To my dear friend and surrogate brother, Bálint Józsa. You are a legend! Thank you for our deep conversations about personal growth and career development and for your contribution to my topic about surrounding ourselves with the right people. Your added distinction will help many, and I love you.

To Dr Marcia Becherel: your emotional breakthrough work has made an irreversible and inspiring difference in my life. Thank you for your service of love and for sharing your healing gift with me on hundreds of occasions over the years. Our journey together into the depths of my psyche and the power of human potential has been profound, to say the least, and I will forever be grateful for your mission, your heart, and your presence in my life.

Thank you to the staff members at the Grand Hyatt in Melbourne, Kiwanda Café, and Café Namoo on Mount Tamborine who served and waited on me as I sat for hours writing this very book. Thank you for your hospitality and care.

To Dr Kim Jobst, for your friendship and unconditional love. Thank you for the many deep, soul-bearing, soul-searching conversations and for helping me find and lean into my edge to discover the truth so I can navigate my way forwards. You have been there in more poignant moments then I can count, and your presence will remain a part of me forever.

To Faith Anderson for reminding me of my greater potential and for knowing without words when I need you most. Bella, I love you. Your soul sister energy lifts me up and I adore the conversations that we have, reflecting on the parallels in our lives and the path of fulfilling our individual purposes here.

Thank you to my production team who helped to bring this book to life including Ursula McCabe for her outstanding editing and proofreading skills, Chandrashekhar Yadav for his service of love with the typesetting and layout, Noel Agravante for his support

Acknowledgements

with the cover design. Thank you also to my dear friend Angelika Jankovic for writing the beautiful Foreword and to Laraib Malik for her valuable feedback on the first draft manuscript.

To every client, friend, fan, follower, customer, or mentor who has ever believed in me or taken a leap of faith to work with me, read my books, or been part of my projects. You are my dream come to life.

And finally, thank you to myself, for not giving up when I was near-suicidal and hitting rock-bottom so many years ago. Your courage to face the challenge and find your way through to the other side was immense. I thank you from the bottom of my heart for being willing to make the most of your life. I know the journey has not always been easy, but please know that I love you and respect you for your stubborn determination and your endless belief in life's possibilities. You deserve the best.

ABOUT THE AUTHOR

Emily Gowor is a self-help writer, author, and keynote speaker. After overcoming near-suicidal depression earlier in her journey, Emily turned her life around and devoted herself and her career to inspiring people to reach for more. She has now spent more than 18 years helping people to achieve their goals and dreams.

As the author of 13 books on the topics of self-help, entrepreneurship, and writing – including *Born Great* and *Reflections on Purpose* – Emily produced an award-winning blog, Life Travels, attracting thousands of readers online. As a speaker, Emily has presented in Australia and abroad, spreading her messages of inspiration and sharing the stage with leaders including Dr John Demartini, international best-selling author and star of *The Secret*.

Emily's writing, speaking, products, and programs have touched thousands of lives globally. Her life-changing programs help people to find and fulfil their purpose in career and business. Extensively trained in human behaviour and personal growth tools and teachings, Emily is Master Certified in NLP (Neuro-Linguistic Programming) and Hypnosis as well as previously being a trained facilitator in the life-changing method of Dr John Demartini.

As a winner of the 2012 and 2014 Anthill 30under30 Young Entrepreneur Award, Emily has been featured in media sharing her messages of encouragement and wisdom, including her appearance on the Global Women Empowerment TV Show in Melbourne, Australia. Having already fulfilled upon a meaningful career, Emily continues to inspire people from around the world to find and fulfil their destiny.

www.emilygowor.com

Other Books By Emily

This inspiring 2-part full-colour guided journal will help you connect with your soul's purpose on Earth. The journal includes Emily's formula for writing a 1-sentence purpose statement, 40 reflective questions about you and your life, the Archetype of Greatness exercise and more! It will awaken the truth about what you were born to do.

Purple hardcover with silver foil & spiral binding

Born Great is an inspirational book that will encourage you to fulfil your destiny. Written in 3 parts – Vision, Wealth & Work – it will guide and encourage you to create the extraordinary life you are capable of. Exploring a wide range of topics from purpose through to our relationship with money and how to turn what you love into a career path, this book will be your companion as you pursue your destiny.

Foreword by Dr John Demartini

Order now at www.emilygowor.com

www.ingramcontent.com/pod-product-compliance
Lightning Source LLC
Chambersburg PA
CBHW062046290426
44109CB00027B/2742